The Authors

KENNETH BOA is Director of Publications and Research for SEARCH Ministries and a seminar teacher with Walk Thru the Bible Ministries. A graduate of Case Institute of Technology and Dallas Theological Seminary, he is a doctoral candidate at New York University. He formerly served as the college pastor and a part-time faculty member at The King's College, Briarcliff Manor, New York. He is the author of *God, I Don't Understand* and *Cults, World Religions, and You* (both by Victor Books), *The Return of the Star of Bethlehem* (Doubleday), *Talk Thru the Old Testament* and *Talk Thru the New Testament* (both by Tyndale), *Seeds of Change* (Crossway), and *Talk Thru the Bible* (Thomas Nelson). He and his wife, Karen, are parents of a daughter, Heather, and live in Roswell, Georgia.

LARRY MOODY is Director of National Services for SEARCH Ministries and also teaches for Walk Thru the Bible Ministries. A graduate of The King's College, he received his master's degree in theology from Dallas Theological Seminary. While a Dallas student, he helped design a follow-up program now published by Zondervan under the title *Eight Vital Relationships for Christian Growth*. He and his wife, Ruth, are parents of Joshua, Daniel, Rebecca, and Deborah and live in Timonium, Maryland.

I'm Glad You Asked

Kenneth Boa & Larry Moody

This book is designed for individual use and also for group study. A Leader's Guide with Victor Multiuse Transparency Masters is available from your local bookstore, SEARCH Ministries, or the publisher. A boxed set of color-coded flash cards that will help you memorize the flow charts and key illustrations in this book is available from the authors at $4.95, postpaid. Address: SEARCH Ministries, 101 W. Ridgely Road, Suite 5A, Lutherville, MD 21093

VICTOR BOOKS®

A DIVISION OF SCRIPTURE PRESS PUBLICATIONS INC.
USA CANADA ENGLAND

8 9 10 Printing/Year 94 93 92

PRODUCED IN
COOPERATION WITH

SEARCH
MINISTRIES

Scripture quotations are from the *New American Standard Bible*
(NASB), © the Lockman Foundation 1960, 1962, 1963, 1968, 1971,
1972, 1973, 1975, 1977.

Recommended Dewey Decimal Classification: 253.4
  Suggested Subject Heading: APOLOGETICS

Library of Congress Catalog Card Number: 82-50619
ISBN: 0-88207-354-0

CONTENTS

Foreword   **8**

1 How to Use This Book   **9**
2 Cultivating Opportunities   **13**
3 Is There Really a God?   **17**
4 Why Believe in Miracles?   **40**
5 Isn't Christianity Just a Psychological Crutch?   **63**
6 How Accurate Is the Bible?   **74**
7 Why Do the Innocent Suffer?   **102**
8 Is Christ the Only Way to God?   **126**
9 Will God Judge Those Who Never Heard about Christ?   **145**
10 If Christianity Is True, Why Are There So Many Hypocrites?   **164**
11 What about Good Works?   **175**
12 Isn't Salvation by Faith Too Simple?   **192**
13 What Does the Bible Mean by *Believe?*   **199**
14 Can Anyone Be Sure of his Salvation?   **208**

Epilogue   **224**
General Bibliography   **226**

To our wives, Karen and Ruth
". . . a woman who fears the Lord, she shall be praised."
Proverbs 31:30

Acknowledgments

Our first acknowledgment must go to Matthew S. Prince. Matt taught us the significance of answering honestly and objectively the skeptical questions of our non-Christian friends. A special thanks to Bill Kraftson, who has faithfully sought to answer these objections through the course of his ministry and whose illustrations and sayings are sprinkled throughout this work. To Dave DeWitt, our fellow laborer in friendship evangelism, for his practical grasp on how to transform each of these objections into an opportunity for others to consider the claims of Christ. To Dave Krueger for his constant encouragement and insights into the charts and material. And to James Duncan, a layman who loves Christ and unbelievers, for his original suggestion to put the questions in a flow chart form.

Foreword

Many centuries ago St. Augustine said, "No one indeed believes anything unless he has first thought that it is to be believed." In fact, the scriptural exhortation is to give "a defense to everyone who asks you to give an account for the hope that is in you . . ." (1 Peter 3:15). The authors of this book are committed to reaching hearts for Christ without insulting minds. In this book they have provided an excellent tool for accomplishing this purpose.

This book is a handbook on evangelism. But unlike many such books it does not concentrate merely on *how* to reach people without providing the reasons *why* they should believe. The authors are conscious not only of *what* we are to share with the world but with *whom* we are sharing it. They are concerned about reaching unsaved intelligent people who may have intelligent questions. In response to this need they have provided intelligent answers to questions that are often asked.

My own experience in evangelizing people for over 30 years confirms the approach taken in this book. It is a simple, clear, and thoughtful approach to evangelism. The application of its principles will yield good results for the cause of the Gospel.

NORMAN L. GEISLER
Professor of Systematic Theology
Dallas Theological Seminary

1
How to Use This Book

How often have you been overwhelmed by an onslaught of tough objections as you attempted to communicate the message of Christianity to your non-Christian friends? It does not take much dialogue before the standard objections begin to emerge:

How can you be sure there really is a God?
What basis is there for believing in miracles?
Isn't Christianity just a psychological crutch for weak people?
The Bible is full of errors and myths—how can you believe it?
If God is good, why do evil and suffering exist?
Isn't it narrow-minded to claim that Christ is the only way to God?
What about people who never heard about Christ—will they be condemned?
How can Christianity be true when its adherents are so phony and hypocritical?
Would God reject people who have lived basically good lives?
Isn't just believing in Christ for salvation too easy?
How much faith do you need to have?
Can anyone be sure he will go to heaven?

These are honest questions that require thoughtful answers, but few Christians are capable of successfully fielding all of them. This book is designed to help you think through the issues involved so that you can become more effective in your defense of the faith.

Christian apologetics—arguments systematically defending the

Christian faith—really has a twofold purpose. Outwardly, it defends the truth of the Christian world view and answers the objections raised by critics. Inwardly, it strengthens the faith of believers by showing that their faith rests upon a firm foundation. We wrote this book with both purposes in mind. The objections we deal with are derived from repeated experience, not theoretical speculation. Many hundreds of hours of conversation with non-Christian friends led us to the conclusion that the same basic objections keep surfacing in individual and group discussions. We have found that these objections can be boiled down to variations and combinations of the 12 questions addressed in chapters 3-14.

"Be Ready"

Many Christians shy away from defending their beliefs or resort to a "just take it by faith" attitude. They think that the burden of apologetics is too great to be shouldered by laymen. But Peter exhorts us to be ready to make a defense when we are asked to do so: "Sanctify Christ as Lord in your hearts, always being ready to make a defense to every one who asks you to give an account for the hope that is in you, yet with gentleness and reverence" (1 Peter 3:15).

It is encouraging to discover that practically the entire range of objections to the Christian world view can be conveniently reduced to a set of one dozen basic questions. Furthermore, every one of these objections is actually a golden opportunity—an opportunity to lead up to a natural presentation of the Gospel. This is why our development in this book of each of these 12 objections leads to a confrontation with the claims of Christ.

Chapters 3-14 can be read in any order. In one sense, they stand on their own. But in another way, they all are interdependent, referring to one another for support. The two pillars upon which most answers rest are the authority of the Bible and the historical resurrection of Jesus Christ. These are developed in chapter 6 and in the appendix to chapter 4, and the rest of the book often refers to these two key chapters.

The 12 questions are arranged from general to specific. The first three are general objections to religion, the next five are objections to Christianity in particular, and the final four are problems specifically related to the way of salvation (see Chart 1).

The flow charts that appear throughout these chapters will help you visualize the basic options to each question and the logical progres-

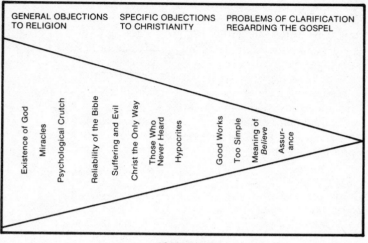

(CHART 1)

sion from one option to another. They have been provided as conceptual guidelines, not straitjackets. It is not necessary or advisable to take a person through all the steps in one of these flow charts when he raises one of these objections. Doing so could be disastrous. Instead, a knowledge of these diagrams (you may want to memorize the basic flow of each chart) can enable you to pinpoint the real issues that need to be addressed. The charts are not designed to bog you down but to give you a freedom in creatively dealing with these questions.

Some of the flow charts include optional material. This will be represented by boxes that are set off to one side.

In Chart 2 you can proceed directly from *a* to *c* to *f*, because the material in boxes *b, d,* and *e* is supplementary. If you find it necessary to deal with issue *d*, you will then have to go to *e* before continuing with *f*.

This book goes into more detail than you will need on any given occasion. Use only what is necessary, and don't try to prove too much. It would be unwise, for example, to discuss the existence of God or to plunge into the problem of evil if a person is ready to personally consider the claims of Christ. Your object is to remove

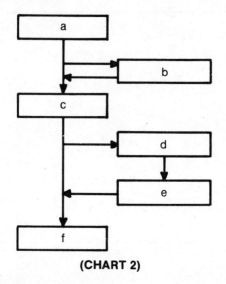

(CHART 2)

barriers to the Gospel as quickly and effectively as possible, and not to exhaustively explore them.

Three Ways People Ask

Keep in mind that people can ask these questions in three different ways. They can be raised as obstacles intended to defeat the Christian position. They can be asked by people who want to "show off" in a group. Or they can be asked out of a real desire to find out the answer, if there is one. A sensitivity to a person's degree of openness will affect the way you handle his question.

We have provided a variety of illustrations to assist you in answering these questions. Illustrations can serve as windows of truth that illuminate concepts by means of analogy. Use the ones you feel comfortable with or create your own.

The supplemental reading at the end of the chapters is limited to fairly brief treatments of these questions. For more detailed reading, consult the bibliography at the conclusion of the book.

We hope *I'm Glad You Asked* will strengthen your confidence in the trustworthiness of God and His Word and further equip you to give an account for the hope that is in you.

2
Cultivating Opportunities

Just knowing the answers to questions non-Christians ask does not guarantee results. Many Christians have made the mistake of dropping answers on people who question Christianity, expecting them immediately to see the light. Little wonder that the Bible uses an agricultural motif to illustrate how people are brought into God's family. There is a period of time between the sowing of the seed (the Gospel) and the harvest of people. But it's unthinkable to sow seed without proper soil preparation, and cultivation must come before the harvest. Much emphasis in evangelism is placed simply on sowing and reaping. The following steps add the very important dimension of preparation and cultivation.

One of the key ways of "cultivating the soil" is *prayer*. Scripture contains many references which describe prayer as essential, but prayer is often ignored in evangelism. Time and time again we have seen that where there was more prayer, there were more results for Christ. As someone has said, "Prayer is striking the winning blow; service is simply gathering up the results."

How to Relate to Non-Christians
In Colossians 4:2-6, Paul explains how the Christian should relate to the non-Christian. As we lay the groundwork through prayer, there are three things the Apostle Paul tells us to do. First, we should *devote* ourselves to prayer, making it a priority, because this is where the battle is won or lost.

13

Second, we must keep alert as we pray. After we have asked God for specific things, we need to watch and see what He will do for us. This means that once we have asked God to open doors to reach others for Christ, we must be alert to these opportunities when they come along.

Third, we are to have a thankful attitude. This implies expectancy. We can be thankful because we expect God to respond to our prayers. "Without faith it is impossible to please Him" (Heb. 11:6).

After giving us three characteristics of prayer, Paul gives us three requests for which we are to pray. First, we need to pray for each other. Many times as Christians we forget that we are in a war, and that we need to uplift one another in prayer. The Apostle Paul, though an outstanding missionary, recognized his own need for prayer.

The second thing that Paul asks us to pray for is an open door with non-Christians. It is unnecessary to beat the fruit off the tree and risk "bruising the fruit" if we have prepared it adequately in prayer. Paul said that we are to pray that the Holy Spirit would go before us and open the door so that the non-Christian will be receptive to what we have to offer. This takes all the pressure off us and puts it on God. It also prevents us from forcing a conversation and turning someone off. We can pray diligently that God will give us an open door or natural opportunity to talk with someone, and then simply wait on God's timing.

The third thing we are to pray for is the grace to present the message clearly when the opportunity presents itself.

Learn from Aristotle

After we have bathed our actions and attitudes in prayer, how else can we cultivate the soil? When Aristotle instructed his pupils on how to win others to their perspective, he noted that they were not to begin by trying to prove that their philosophical view was correct. Rather, they would first have to prove themselves trustworthy. After they won the trust of others, these young philosophers were to consider the problems facing the people they sought to reach. Once they accomplished both of these objectives, the students could then show how their philosophy fulfilled the practical needs of their friends. This principle is also valid in transmitting the message of Christ.

Sometimes Christians share Christ for the wrong reasons. Some bear witness of Christ so they can proudly display their converts like scalps hung from their spiritual belts. Others witness out of guilt, doing it more to soothe their own conscience than to benefit the people they approach.

As we share Christ with others, it is important to demonstrate a genuine *love* for them. J. I. Packer stressed this in his book, *Evangelism and the Sovereignty of God* (InterVarsity):

It must never be forgotten that the enterprise required of us in evangelism is the enterprise of love: an enterprise that springs from a genuine interest in those whom we seek to win, and a genuine care for their well-being, and expresses itself in a genuine respect for them and a genuine friendliness towards them (pp. 79-80).

Christ called us to have an unconditional love for our non-Christian friends. Friendships are fragile and require as much care in handling as any other fragile and precious thing. A person must trust you before he will be willing to examine your product. Abraham Lincoln once said, "If you would win a man to your cause, first convince him that you are his true friend. Therein is a drop of honey which will catch his heart—which, say what you will, is the greater high road to his reason. When you have once gained his heart, you have little trouble convincing his judgment of the justices of your cause, if indeed that cause is really just."

Once a person recognizes your sincere concern for him and realizes that what you offer stems from a heart of love, he will respond far more readily. But not only must we love a person, we must also *listen* to what he has to say. Someone once said, "Christ is the answer; now what's your question?" Having listened to his objections, you can more easily expose him to the reality of Christ. An important aspect of communication is listening.

A student once approached the noted Harvard scholar Charles T. Copeland and asked, "Why are there no courses in conversation? Is there anything I can do to learn the art of conversation?"

"Of course there is," answered Copeland, "and if you'll just listen, I'll tell you what it is."

There ensued a long and awkward silence until the student finally exclaimed, "Well, I'm listening."

"You see," said Copeland triumphantly, "you are learning already!"

After exposing people to a Christlike love, we prove ourselves trustworthy. Then having examined their objections and needs by listening intently to their conversation, we can lead them toward a consideration of the claims of Christ. When seeking to explain the message of Christ, it is important to communicate clearly. The Good News should be expressed clearly so they will appreciate it, picturesquely so they will remember it, and above all, accurately so they will be guided by its light. We have sought to follow these guidelines in the following chapters to enable you to present a cogent message to those searching for solid answers.

God has called us to sow, cultivate, and reap. But it is not an instantaneous process. With some people, we may only sow or cultivate or reap. What we must keep before us is the commission of Christ to be faithful to the task no matter what stage of the cycle we are in.

Finally, our confidence must never be in the answers we offer, but in the convicting ministry of the Holy Spirit (John 16:8-11). We must walk in conscious dependence on His power working through us, or our efforts will be worthless. People often raise these objections as excuses to avoid a confrontation with Christ. Even if we successfully overcome their objections, they will not come to Christ unless they are drawn by the Spirit.

3

Is There Really a God?

Often-Asked Questions:

Can you actually prove that God exists?

Since God's existence cannot be proved, isn't agnosticism the most reasonable position?

Hasn't science demonstrated that the idea of a God is unnecessary?

Why postulate a God when evolution explains the origin of life and man?

Three Options

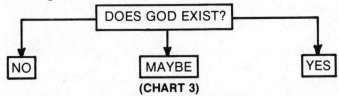

(CHART 3)

The options are simple—one must believe that God does *not* exist (atheism), God *may* exist (agnosticism), or God *does* exist (see Chart 3). But even if the third option is believed to be true, there is still the problem of what kind of God a person has in mind. Is it impersonal, or is He personal? This question is not fully answered until the non-Christian is confronted with the infinite, personal, and ethical God of the Bible.

17

First Option: God Does Not Exist*

If a person begins with a *No*, it will be necessary not only to overcome the objection of atheism but also to take him through the *Maybe* before arriving at the *Yes*. In most cases, the attempt to move a thinking person directly from a *No* to a *Yes* would be unwise.

Begin by drawing a large circle to represent the entire scope of knowledge (see Chart 4). Then ask your friend to symbolize his knowledge in comparison to all knowledge. Even the most arrogant person would be compelled to draw a tiny circle.

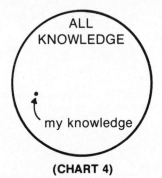

(CHART 4)

We all use only a small percentage of our total mental capacity, but even if we could draw on 100 percent, our knowledge would be paltry when compared to all that could be known. Therefore, it is completely unreasonable to say, "I *know* that God does not exist." A person would have to know everything before that statement could be confirmed.

Missionaries have had difficulty describing ice to natives in equatorial regions. The more they talked about cubes of water or water that became so solid that people could easily walk on it, the harder the natives laughed. Ice was outside their sphere of knowl-

---

*Some of the concepts in this chapter are more involved than in the other chapters. For example, the authors delve into the science of physics and draw on philosophical arguments to answer this question. If you get bogged down, just extract the essence of this chapter without covering every point. The authors have included the more complex sections for readers who want to carry their study a little further. However, this is the only chapter in which you should have any problem.—EDITOR

edge, but this did not jeopardize its existence. Similarly, a person may deny the existence of God, but he must be omniscient to logically do so. Ironically, one would have to be God to be sure that God does not exist. In addition, those who deny God are actually repressing the awareness God has given them (see Rom. 1:18-21).

Before discussing the second option with a questioner, it is sometimes good to help him think his way through the implications of a universe with no God. The human heart cries out for meaning, value, and purpose, but these are precisely the things that are denied in an atheistic cosmos. The universe is expanding, and left to itself, the galaxies will grow farther apart and the stars will eventually burn out. All will be cold, dark, and lifeless. On the scale of cosmic time, the human race (let alone the life of a man) flashes into existence for the briefest moment before passing into oblivion. From an ultimate standpoint, all that we do is meaningless—no one will be left to remember in the endless cosmic night.

Also, without God we have no basis for morality, meaning that values such as right and wrong and good and bad are totally relative and have no absolute mooring. If man is the product of an accidental combination of molecules in an ultimately impersonal universe, human values such as honesty, brotherhood, love, and equality have no more cosmic significance than treachery, selfishness, hatred, and prejudice.

Man is also stripped of purpose in a godless reality. An impersonal universe is bereft of purpose and plan; in the final analysis it moves only toward decay, disorder, and death. It is Macbeth's "tale told by an idiot, full of sound and fury, signifying nothing." In such a pointless existence, human aspirations are mocked by silence.

Not many people have come to grips with these logical implications of atheism, and no one can live consistently with them. All of us *act* as though human existence has meaning, as though moral values are real, and as though human life has purpose and dignity. But all these things presuppose an infinite-personal Creator, so if God is dead, man is also as good as dead.

Before moving to the second option, see Chart 5 for the first.

Second Option: God May Exist
There is a growing climate of opinion that modern science has filled in the gaps that were previously occupied by God, thus rendering the

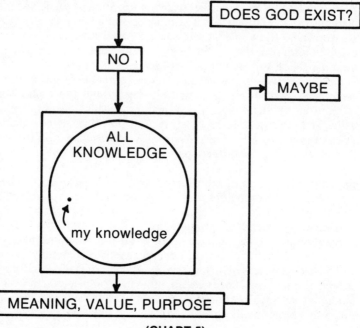

(CHART 5)

existence of God unnecessary. In some circles, agnosticism has been elevated to the status of an intellectual virtue.

Can we prove that God exists? There has been a great deal of debate over the value of theistic arguments, but it is clear that if a person is intellectually or spiritually closed to the question, he will not respond to the evidence. It has been said that "a man persuaded against his will is of the same opinion still." But if a person is willing to consider the case for God's existence, he will find that the evidence consistently points to the *Yes* conclusion.

As we look at the second option, we must overcome some misconceptions about the meaning of "proof." What kind of proof is necessary and how much? Some people wrongly demand scientific proof for the reality of God, as though He could somehow be found at the end of a repeatable and controlled experiment. Russian cosmonaut Yuri Gagarin illustrated this mentality when he returned from orbiting the earth and said, "I didn't see any God out there." This is somewhat like scraping the paint off a portrait to find the artist inside. The painting points to the artist just as the cosmos points to a Creator, but we must remember that the Creator is distinct from His creation.

The scientific method of controlled and repeatable experimentation is useful for achieving a great deal of knowledge: smoking increases the probability of lung cancer, a molecule of water consists of two hydrogen atoms and one oxygen atom, the earth orbits the sun, etc. But there are other kinds of knowledge (historical knowledge, philosophical knowledge, moral knowledge, personal knowledge, religious knowledge), and these lie outside the scope of scientific inquiry.

Verdicts in courts of law are based on legal historical proof, not scientific proof. In civil cases the verdict is reached on the basis of a preponderance of the credible evidence. In criminal cases the jury must be convinced of guilt "beyond a reasonable doubt" before reaching the verdict of guilty. The phrase is *not* "beyond the shadow of a doubt" because 100 percent proof is rarely attainable. If complete proof were required before making legal verdicts or personal decisions, practically nothing would be accomplished.

There is a danger of demanding so much evidence that people become immune to the evidence that is already before them. "If they do not listen to Moses and the Prophets, neither will they be persuaded if someone rises from the dead" (Luke 16:31). God's existence cannot be demonstrated to another person with the kind of certainty that forces him to believe. The evidence may be powerful, but one must choose to respond. This is where faith comes in, not against the evidence but as a response to it. Belief in God is not a leap into the dark, but a step into the light.

Take the story of Bill who was involved in a serious automobile accident. He was brought to an emergency room; as he slowly regained consciousness, he was convinced that he had died and gone to heaven. When the doctor said, "I'll have to operate because of your internal injuries," Bill said, "No, I'm already dead. My car collided head-on with that truck, and there's no way I could have escaped death."

The doctor tried to no avail to persuade him that he was really in the hospital and should will to pull through the operation. Then an idea popped into his mind: "Bill, do you know that dead men don't bleed?"

"Yes, I know that."

"Then if I cut your finger and it starts to bleed, will you admit that you're alive?"

"Sure," Bill replied.

So, in desperation, the doctor cut Bill's finger and when Bill saw the blood coming out, he paused and said thoughtfully, "Son of a gun—dead men *do* bleed!"

A decision must be based on sufficient evidence, not exhaustive evidence. But what constitutes sufficient evidence for the existence of God? Because God is not perceived by our five senses, we must rely upon the indirect evidence of *cause and effect*. We depend on this kind of inferential reasoning every day, and this is the kind of reasoning that will point us in the direction of God as well. A sufficient *cause* must exist to account for the *effects* of the natural universe, order and design within the universe, personal beings, and the phenomenon of morality.

The philosophers Leibniz and Sartre argued that the most basic philosophical question is "Why is there something rather than nothing?" Why does anything exist at all? There are only four possible answers to this question, and our purpose in taking an agnostic through these options is to help him see that the universe is contingent—it depends on something else for its existence.

Four Alternatives

This brings us to the *If Proposition:* If anything now exists, something must be eternal, or else something not eternal must have emerged from nothing. Here are the four alternatives we must examine: (1) the universe is an illusion, (2) the universe is eternal, (3) the universe emerged from nothing, and (4) the universe was created by an eternal Being.

(1) *The universe is an illusion.* This is a self-defeating position, equivalent to saying "It is an objective fact that there are no objective facts." The claim that all things are unreal lacks logical consistency, because the claim itself would also be unreal. The following sentence falls into the same category: "This sentence is incorrect." The sentence is self-defeating, because it must be false in order to be true.

Not only does this option lack rational coherence, it also lacks factual correspondence. To entertain it, a person would have to reject every shred of evidence from his five senses. If it is an illusion, the universe is a very powerful, relentless, and consistent fantasy. We are constantly being bombarded by sensory data that can be used to make reliable predictions (tides, planetary orbits, etc.). Furthermore, no human being can live consistently with the implications of this viewpoint for even a day. Even the full-blown skeptic looks both ways before crossing the street. And every human relationship calls illusionism a lie.

(2) *The universe is eternal.* In this case, the something that must be eternal in the If Proposition is the universe itself. If this is so, the universe accounts for its own existence. It is not contingent because it is infinitely old. There are three scientific reasons why this position is now unacceptable.

The first reason comes from the latest evidence concerning cosmogony, i.e., the origin of the universe. Until recently, the theory that the universe had no beginning and that matter is eternal was quite popular among scientists. When new discoveries began to threaten this theory, many scientists tried to salvage it (sometimes because of antisupernatural motives) by retreating into the *steady-state theory,* which holds that the universe has always existed in a state of relative equilibrium.

Astronomer Fred Hoyle even postulated that this equilibrium is maintained by "continuous creation" of background hydrogen atoms. The basic question, of course, is where this created material comes from. Hoyle answered, "It does not come from anywhere. Material appears—it is created." This is an incredible leap of faith, since it violates the most basic principle of physics, the law of conservation of mass and energy. Little wonder that Hoyle later abandoned this theory.

The discovery by Edwin Hubble that the universe is uniformly expanding in all directions led George Gamow to trace this process back into the past until he reached a point where all matter was compressed into an unimaginably dense and hot primordial "atom." Gamow's *big-bang theory* holds that this atom exploded immediately after creation, eventually resulting in the present expanding universe. The additional discovery in 1965 of an omnidirectional background radiation in the universe forced the vast majority of astronomers to accept the big-bang theory because it supports the conclusion that the universe was once dense and hot. All this is extremely significant, because this widely held model says that the whole universe had a definite beginning a finite time ago. And if, as this theory implies, the universe emerged from a point that was infinitely dense, this would really mean that space, time, matter, and energy appeared out of nothing.

Some astronomers have attempted to avoid the theological implications of the big-bang theory by suggesting that we are in a pulsating universe which is going through an endless series of expansions and contractions. For the universe to oscillate in this way, it would have to be "closed." That is, there must be enough gravitational force to stop the expansion and pull all matter back together. But the evidence points to an "open" universe that will never stop expanding. To be closed, the universe would have to be about 10 times more dense than it is. (Even if the universe were closed, the first contraction would probably implode with such gravitational force that a giant black hole would be produced from which no matter or light could escape. And if *this* were not the case, each successive universal expansion would be significantly larger than the one before. Thus, even a closed universe points back to a beginning.)

The second scientific reason why the universe is not eternal is the present abundance of hydrogen in the cosmos. Throughout the universe, hydrogen is being converted into helium through the process of nuclear fusion in the cores of the stars. This process is irreversible, and new hydrogen is not being formed in any significant amounts by the breakdown of heavier atoms. Thus, an infinitely old universe would mean that there should be almost no hydrogen left. Yet most of the universe is made up of hydrogen.

The third reason that the universe had a beginning is the second law of thermodynamics. The *first* law of thermodynamics is the law of conservation of mass and energy: mass and energy are interchangeable, but they cannot be created or destroyed. The energy equivalence of mass can be found by using Einstein's equation $E=mc^2$. We will call this mass equivalence. Graphically, the first law looks like Chart 6.

"Density" is added to show that these laws would be true even if the universe were infinite. Regardless of time, the *quantity* of energy and mass equivalence in the universe is a constant. But the *second* law says that the *quality* of energy in the universe is constantly declining.

"Entropy" refers to the amount of useless or random energy in any

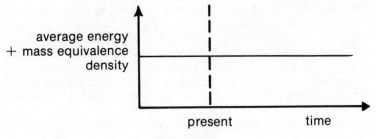

(CHART 6)

closed system. As entropy increases, the amount of useful energy decreases. For example, when a chair is pushed across a floor, the work energy turns into heat energy and heats the floor molecules slightly due to friction. This heat energy in the floor cannot be reorganized to perform work (i.e., move the chair again) and becomes lost. Energy did not disappear, but it became more random and incapable of being used again.

Entropy can also be seen as a measure of disorder, because anything left to itself (a closed system) moves toward a state of equilibrium and randomness. The universe as a whole can be viewed as an immense closed system. (Don't confuse this with a closed universe, i.e., a universe that will eventually stop expanding and begin to contract.) As time increases, universal entropy increases (see Chart 7).

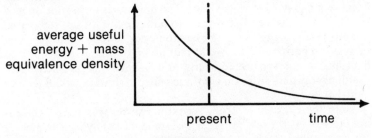

(CHART 7)

The area below the curved line (an exponential decay curve) is useful energy. As time increases, this useful energy approaches zero. Ultimately, a state of equilibrium will be approached, often called the "heat death" of the universe. The stars will have burned out and there will not be enough gas in the steadily expanding galaxies to form new stars. In effect, the universe will have run down like a clock with no one to wind it back up. All will be coldness, darkness, and disorder. (This process is irreversible apart from the intervention of a supernatural agent—God. Romans 8:20-22 describes the future redemption of nature when God sets it free from its "slavery to corruption.")

When these two laws are superimposed graphically, they look like this:

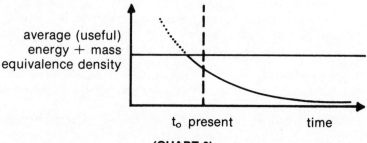

(CHART 8)

In Chart 8 point t_0 represents the time when the curved line (second law) intersected the horizontal line (first law). The curved line is dotted before that time because there cannot be more useful energy than total energy. It is clear that the universe cannot be infinitely old because it has not yet worn down. The only other viable option is to say that the universe existed prior to point t_0. But for this to be true, the universe prior to that point had to be perfectly sustained with no increase in entropy. This would require an omnipresent agent that continually removed useless energy and disorder and replaced it with useful energy and order on a cosmic scale. In short, it would require God Himself.

Thus, there are three strong scientific reasons why the universe is not eternal: (1) the big-bang, (2) the abundance of hydrogen, and (3) the irreversible decay of the universe. Of course, this is not absolute proof, for one could argue that new discoveries will be made that will somehow invalidate these conclusions. But this is a completely hollow faith, because it is contrary to all the evidence.

There are also philosophical reasons why there cannot have been an actually infinite series of events in time, but the scientific reasons should be sufficient. For those interested, these philosophical reasons are nicely developed in William Lane Craig's little book, *The Existence of God and the Beginning of the Universe* (Here's Life Publishers).

(3) *The universe emerged from nothing.* Little needs to be said about the absurdity of this position. All reason and observations tell us that nothing produces nothing. To say that an effect can exist without a cause is to deny the whole basis of scientific investigation and rational thought. No one would seriously maintain that a house, planet, star, or galaxy simply popped into existence without a cause. Yet some are willing to strain at these gnats while swallowing the camel that the entire universe came into an uncaused existence out of nothing. For this is exactly what the atheist who accepts the big-bang theory is forced to believe.

(4) *The universe was created by an eternal Being.* This is the only option left if the universe is real, not eternal, and caused. The universe is an effect which is contingent on a cause that is beyond it. The only sufficient cause is an eternal and necessary Being—someone or something incapable of *not* being, whether or not anything else exists. Otherwise, there would be the problem of an infinite regression of causes and effects. Therefore, the old question, "Who caused God?" is as nonsensical as, "Who made the unmakable being?" God is eternal and self-existent; He always exists and cannot cease to exist. It is true that every effect must have a cause, but God is *not* an effect because He was never created. (The concept of self-existence is not the same as self-creation. Nothing could create itself because it would have to exist prior to its existence to do so!) So we are left with an eternal Being as the only viable solution to the If Proposition.

Chart 9 shows the second option to the "Does God exist?" question.

Third Option: God Does Exist

So far we have used cause-and-effect reasoning to conclude that the natural universe points beyond itself to an eternal Being for the cause of its existence. This is a *cosmological argument* for the existence of God because it is based on evidence from the whole cosmos. But this argument is limited, because it does not prove that this eternal Being is the personal God revealed in the Bible.

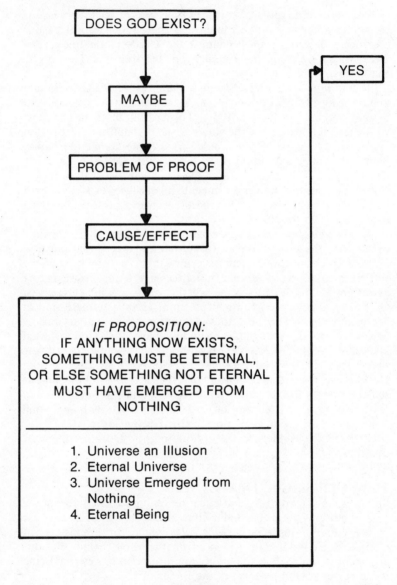

DOES GOD EXIST?

MAYBE

PROBLEM OF PROOF

CAUSE/EFFECT

IF PROPOSITION:
IF ANYTHING NOW EXISTS,
SOMETHING MUST BE ETERNAL,
OR ELSE SOMETHING NOT ETERNAL
MUST HAVE EMERGED FROM
NOTHING

1. Universe an Illusion
2. Eternal Universe
3. Universe Emerged from
   Nothing
4. Eternal Being

YES

(CHART 9)

When a person is willing to admit the existence of some kind of eternal Being or God, the next question is whether this Being is impersonal or personal. To answer this question, we need to narrow our focus from the universe as a whole to specific aspects of creation. What cause is sufficient to explain the effects of order and design in the universe, the personality of man, and the moral consciousness of man?

Before looking at the argument from design, note that even the cosmological argument favors a personal over an impersonal cause of the cosmos. If an impersonal cause always existed, why did the universe come into existence only a finite time ago? What kept the cause from producing the effect (the universe) an eternity ago? It certainly couldn't be an act of the will. Only a personal Being could make the choice to create the universe a limited time ago.

Now we are ready to look beyond the *fact* of the temporal universe to the *form* of the universe. We live in a universe of order, complexity, and symmetry, not a multiverse of chaos and confusion. The whole scientific enterprise is built upon the assumption that the universe is orderly and predictable. We can find thousands of examples of order and purpose in the world, especially in living systems. This is the argument from design, also known as the *teleological argument* from the Greek word *telos,* meaning end or goal.

If we examined a radio, we would find that its component parts are all designed to work together to accomplish a specific function. The more we understand the principles of electronics and how components such as transistors, capacitors, resistors, and transformers work in accordance with those principles, the more we can appreciate the purposeful intelligence and creative design required to make a radio. Yet a radio is only child's play when compared to the enormous complexity and subtlety of a living cell. Biologists are only beginning to realize how profound living systems really are, and yet many people still cling tightly to the theory that, given enough time, this design can be produced by chance.

Those who place their faith in atheistic evolution must maintain the philosophically absurd position that chaos produced order, lifeless matter produced life, chance produced intelligence, and accidents produced purpose. It is nonsense to say that an effect can be greater than its cause. This is why these people spell nature with a capital N and slip intelligent purpose (teleology) through the back door under the guise of "natural selection." In this way, the evolutionary process itself becomes a substitute god in a universe that would otherwise be utterly impersonal. (See the appendix on evolution at the end of this chapter.)

In all areas of life we think teleologically—we assume purpose and order when we encounter other minds and when we interpret the data perceived by our senses. Why abandon this consistent principle when looking at the design in the universe as a whole?

An even stronger evidence for the personality of the Creator is the personality of man. Personality refers to man's intellect, emotion, and will. The basic issue in this *anthropological argument* is once again cause and effect: The impersonal has no ability to think, feel, or choose and is, therefore, vastly inferior to that which is personal. How, then, can an impersonal agent cause conscious, personal beings? We can strengthen this argument by looking in more detail at the three basic areas of personality. The three qualities of intellect, feeling, and will, form the basis for the arguments from thought, aesthetics, and morality.

The argument from *thought* shows that the human mind cannot be the product of an impersonal process. It is self-defeating to argue that the mind is merely the physical brain, an organic electrochemical mechanism which evolved as a result of irrational causes. To do so would be to use human reasoning to question the validity of human reasoning. This is like trying to prove that there are no proofs.

Human thought transcends the brain and the material world as it reflects upon abstract concepts like justice, wisdom, and spirit. We cannot only think about the future, but we can also think about the process of thinking about the future.

The argument from *aesthetics* appeals to a personal God as the only adequate explanation of the universal aesthetic experience in man. While there are differences in taste, there is, nevertheless, an amazing amount of consensus concerning beauty and greatness in art, literature, music, architecture, and so forth. This awareness and appreciation of what is beautiful cannot be reduced to a mechanical response to sensory input. The aesthetic capacity transcends the material world, and an impersonal force is insufficient to create this transcendent quality.

The argument from *morality* holds that man's moral consciousness requires a personal God to have any ultimate meaning. Like aesthetic experience, moral experience is a universal human phenomenon. There are variations, but in all ages and countries, qualities like honesty, wisdom, courage, and fairness are regarded as virtues. Even if a person claims that moral notions are the subjective products of cultural conditioning, he betrays himself every time he criticizes or praises. If a skeptic says, "How could you be so selfish?" he is really appealing to an objective moral standard: consideration for the needs of others. Otherwise, his criticism has no weight. For moral experience to be valid (and all of us live as though it is), it must be based on more than individual or group preferences. Groups and societies can pursue paths as evil as those followed by any individual. The only absolute foundation for morality is the changeless character of the personal Creator of the universe. Righteousness, love, justice, and mercy find their true basis in the personality of God. These qualities have no ultimate significance if the universe is the product of impersonal causes.

Putting all these arguments together, we are left with an eternal, personal, and ethical God as the only sufficient cause of the universe, order and design within the universe, and the personality of man. We saw earlier that no one can live consistently with a philosophy that rules out meaning, value, and purpose in life. We long for these things because we were made to find them all in the infinite-personal God who makes them real. We are not merely biological entities; we are spiritual creatures, made as the image of God and designed to receive and display His life.

Again, these arguments do not provide the kind of absolute proof that will overwhelm a person who chooses to reject God. But they can help a nonmilitant agnostic recognize the reasonableness of faith in God. They can also make him aware of the danger of straddling the fence between rejecting and accepting God.

Suppose a doctor told you that you were afflicted with a disease that would take your life if left untreated. You have a 50-50 chance if he operates. Shaken up, you seek two other opinions and they both concur. Now the choice is up to you, but you can only defer your decision for so long. You would no doubt choose the operation, because a possible solution is better than no solution at all.

Nondecision agnosticism is even more foolish than an indefinite postponement of the operation, because the chances are greater and the stakes are higher. If God exists, agnosticism is eternally unwise.

The agnostic gains nothing and loses everything.

From a biblical perspective, agnosticism is not simply an intellectual process of reserving judgment. It is really a suppression of the truth that God has implanted within the human heart: "For the wrath of God is revealed from heaven against all ungodliness and unrighteousness of men, who suppress the truth in unrighteousness, because that which is known about God is evident within them; for God made it evident to them" (Rom. 1:18-19). This is a *moral,* not merely an intellectual issue. The evidence is not only internal, but as we have been arguing, it is also external: "For since the creation of the world His invisible attributes, His eternal power and divine nature, have been clearly seen, being understood through what has been made, so that they are without excuse. For even though they knew God, they did not honor Him as God, or give thanks; but they became futile in their speculations, and their foolish heart was darkened"(Rom. 1:20-21).

The arguments in this chapter will not be effective unless the Holy Spirit overcomes the natural rebellion in the unbeliever's heart. The non-Christian's responsibility is to respond with faith to the convicting ministry of the Holy Spirit. "And without faith it is impossible to please Him, for he who comes to God must believe that He is, and that He is a rewarder of those who seek Him" (Heb. 11:6).

When a person acknowledges the existence of the infinite and personal God, he must then come to know this God in a personal way. At this point, he needs to be confronted with the claims and credentials of Jesus Christ (see Chapter 8).

Jesus is the Creator of the cosmos, the divine Word who became flesh and came to earth in the likeness of men. "No man has seen God at any time; the only begotten God, who is in the bosom of the Father, He has explained Him" (John 1:18). By looking at the person and work of Jesus Christ, we see the person and the character of God.

The presentation of the claims and credentials of Christ should be followed by an explanation of the Gospel and what it means to believe in Christ (see Chapter 13).

Chart 10 shows the third option to this question.

Summary and Flow Chart

Atheism is unreasonable because a person would have to be omniscient to know that God does not exist. In addition, if there were

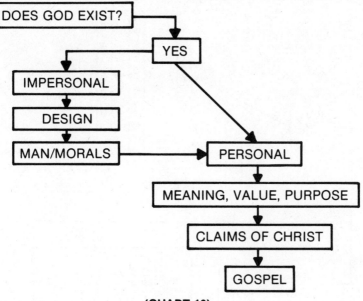

(CHART 10)

no God, human life would be stripped of ultimate meaning, value, and purpose. Agnosticism is not as unreasonable, but the agnostic needs to realize that the weight of the evidence is in favor of theism. No absolute proof can be offered which will force the skeptic to believe against his will, but a strong case can be built by applying cause and effect reasoning to the universe, the order and design in the universe, and the personality of man (thought, aesthetics, and morality). The argument from the universe is designed to show that the universe is not eternal and is, therefore, contingent on an eternal Being for its existence. This Being must be personal, because an impersonal creating agent could not account for human thought and morality. Those who question God's existence must suppress the internal and external testimony that their Creator has given them (Rom. 1:18-21). The clearest manifestation of God in human history was the Incarnation of Jesus Christ, who is the Mediator between God and men.

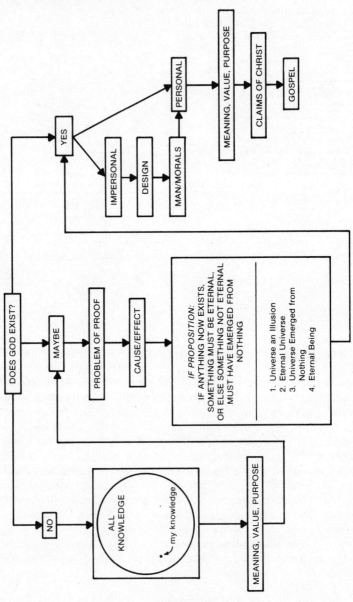

(CHART 11)

Supplemental Reading

(1) Oliver R. Barclay, *Reasons for Faith* (InterVarsity Press). Includes a clear argument for the existence of God the Creator.

(2) Colin Chapman, *Christianity on Trial* (Tyndale House). A good source of quotations by non-Christians on the issues of meaning, value, and purpose.

(3) William Lane Craig, *The Existence of God and the Beginning of the Universe* (Here's Life). Very good material on the If Proposition.

(4) Arlie J. Hoover, *The Case for Christian Theism* (Baker). Chapters 1, 4, 6, 7 are helpful on the issues of atheism, proof, and the theistic arguments.

(5) R. C. Sproul, *If There Is a God, Why Are There Atheists?* (Bethany Fellowship). A fine presentation of the psychology of atheism.

(6) R. C. Sproul, *Objections Answered* (Regal Books). Chapter 7 gives a succinct case for the existence of the eternal God.

Appendix on Evolution

Everyone who believes the Bible accepts the fact that God is the Creator of the universe. But while evangelicals agree on the *who*, they do not all agree on the *how* of creation. Many believe that this is a young earth and that the six days of creation in Genesis 1 are 24-hour days. Others believe that these days are figurative, and that God directly intervened at various points in the long evolutionary process.

The question here is not who is right, but how to deal with the issue of evolution when the non-Christian raises it as an objection to the existence of God or the reliability of the Genesis Creation account. You should deal with this question as quickly as possible so that it will not become a barrier to the discussion about God or the Bible. Resist the temptation of trying to prove too much. You may believe the earth is young, but the more basic issue is nontheistic evolution versus creation by God (regardless of the method and time He used).

The nontheistic evolutionary model assumes that nonliving systems generated life by means of time plus chance, and that microevolution (small changes) leads to macroevolution (large changes, as in the microbe-to-man theory). As we said earlier, the philosophical problem with this model is that it makes the effects (complexity, life, intelligence, personality) greater than the causes (disorder, nonlife, random interactions and mutations, and impersonal events).

There are also scientific problems with nontheistic evolution. It offers no workable mechanism that will account for the first living cell, let alone the complexity of the human brain.

The chemical production of a first living cell would have to follow this sequence: (1) Random atoms must be formed into amino acids. (2) These amino acids must link together to form chains (polypeptides). (3) These chains must become long (hundreds of amino acids) and they must form in an ordered sequence, since there are 20 kinds of amino acids. This will produce a simple protein molecule. (4) More complex proteins must be produced. (5) Very long and highly ordered molecular chains known as DNA must be formed and maintained. (6) An enormously complex chemical factory must be produced, complete with special protein formations, enzymes, DNA, RNA, ribosomes, a cell wall, etc. This single cell must be able to reproduce itself and carry on all the functions of life.

Without a rational ordering agent, every step but the first would require nothing short of a statistical miracle, even under the most ideal circumstances.

Many people argue that, given enough time, even the most improbable events become probable. This sounds reasonable only until specific numbers are used. Let's consider George Bernard Shaw's argument that if a million monkeys constantly typed on a million typewriters for a long enough time, one of them would eventually pound out a Shakespearean play. Assume a million monkeys typing 24 hours a day at 100 words a minute on typewriters with 40 keys. If each word of the play contained four letters, the first word would be typed by one of the monkeys in about 12 seconds. However, it would require about five days to get the first two words (eight letters) on one of the typewriters. How long would it take to get the first four words? About 100 billion years! No one could imagine the amount of time which would be required to produce the first scene.

Beginning with the first step, many evolutionists assume a primordial earthly atmosphere with no oxygen so that amino acids could be formed. However, the very atmosphere that could produce them would immediately lead to their destruction (due to ultraviolet light penetrating this oxygen-free atmosphere) unless they were protected. Unfounded assumptions must be multiplied to overcome this problem.

On the next level, let us assume an ideal environment with a primordial soup full of amino acids and the proper catalysts, with just the right temperature and moisture. Some estimate that under these favorable conditions the chances of getting dipeptides (two amino acids bonded) would be about 1 in 100. But the chances of tripeptide formation would be about 1 in 10,000. To get a polypeptide of only 10 amino acids, the probability would be 1 chance in 100,000,000,000,-000,000,000 (100 quintillion). Yet the proteins in the simplest living things have chains of at least 400 amino acids on the average.

To make matters worse, all proteins are built of amino acids that are exclusively "left-handed" in their molecular orientation. Left-handed and right-handed amino acids are mirror images of each other, and their chances of formation are about the same. Although both kinds can link with each other, the first living systems must have been built with left-handed components only. Some scientists have evoked natural selection here, but this only applies to systems that can already reproduce themselves. Without an intelligent ordering agent, we have only chance to explain this amazing phenomenon. For a chain of 400 left-handed amino acids, the odds would be roughly equivalent to tossing an ordinary coin and coming up with tails 400 times in a row. The chances for that would be approximately 1 in 10^{120} (a 1 followed by 120 zeroes). All this for *one* protein molecule, and hundreds of similar molecules would be needed in the first living system.

None of this accounts for the fact that the 20 kinds of amino acids operate like letters in an alphabet, and they must link in a meaningful sequence to form a usable protein. A random sequence of amino acids would be utterly useless.

DNA is far more complex than any of this, and it too is built out of a highly organized alphabet. The letters are molecules called nucleotides. A cell contains a chain of about three billion pairs of these nucleotides (each gene has about 1,200 nucleotide pairs). The order of these nucleotides or bases is crucial because every triplet of bases along this immense chain is a word. Each word stands for one of the 20 kinds of amino acids. Using these words the DNA can literally create any kind of protein that the cell needs.

The amount of time required to synthesize even one gene (a paragraph of these words) has been calculated by some scientists using absurdly generous assumptions. Using a variation on a well-known illustration, suppose a bird came once every billion years and removed only one atom from a stone the size of the solar system. The amount of time required for the stone to be worn to nothing would be negligible compared to the time needed to create a useful gene by chance, even accounting for chemical affinities and an ideal environment. Shaw's monkeys would long since have pounded out the words of Shakespeare!

But none of this can compare to the *far greater* complexity of a living cell. Even the simplest living system would require elaborately coded information, growth, reproduction, stability, adaptability, environmental response, and metabolism. Yet evolutionists demand spontaneous generation of life through chemical interaction because they think the only other option would be a miracle. In reality, a miracle cannot be avoided. The only question is whether life appeared out of the primordial soup or by the living God.

In addition, none of the above considers the fact that every chemical reaction along the way from amino acids to life is reversible. This means that whenever a higher point of complexity is reached, it is unstable compared to its environment and may break down into its components. A polypeptide bond of four amino acids can easily break down into four separate amino acids.

We mentioned the second law of thermodynamics in connection with the age of the universe. This same fundamental law tells us that all natural processes cause a net increase in entropy (disorder) and a net loss of useful energy. Any system left to itself will decay and degenerate. Free energy from the sun can cause slight increases in complexity, but the breakdown rate soon matches the buildup rate. The only way to build structures as complex as protein is to have an already existing machine that can translate raw energy into a more highly organized form. Solar energy may be plentiful, but it is useless for building complex systems unless such systems already exist. Life comes only from life, complexity only from complexity. Faith in an original spontaneous generation of life goes against all experience and evidence.

It has been said that "teleology is a lady without whom no biologist can exist; yet he is ashamed to be seen with her in public." Design requires a designer, and this is precisely what is lacking in nontheistic evolution.

Of course, the subject of evolution entails other matters such as mutations and natural selection, comparative anatomy, the fossil record, and fossil men. These are not trivial matters, but all we are trying to do in relation to the question about God's existence is show that the impersonal mechanism of evolution will not by itself produce life or personality. Whether or not God superintended any kind of evolutionary process is an entirely different issue and need not be raised to answer this question.

4

Why Believe in Miracles?

Often-Asked Questions:

How can a rational person today accept the stories of miracles in the Bible?

Aren't miracles contrary to the laws of modern science?

There is no historical basis for the miracles in the Bible—aren't they simply myths and legends designed to create religious faith?

If there were miracles then, why doesn't God perform miracles today?

Three Options

(CHART 12)

The first optional answer flatly denies even the possibility of miracles. The assumption is they cannot and, therefore, do not take place. The second option grants that God could perform miracles but questions whether He has chosen to do so. According to this view, the evidence is insufficient to settle the issue, or it is unreasonable to expect that Almighty God would stoop to the use of miracles to cause people to believe in Him. The third option is that God has intervened in history in miraculous ways to accomplish His purposes (see Chart 12).

One of the unique features of Christianity is that its teachings are built directly upon God's miraculous acts on behalf of His people. In most other religions, there are very few accounts of miracles, and these are veiled in mythology. Miracles are more prominent in the scriptures of Hinduism, yet even Hinduism does not crumble if its miracles are removed. But the miracles of the Bible are firmly embedded in space-time history, and the truth of Christianity stands or falls with the historicity of these miracles, especially the Resurrection. Passages such as John 10:25; 14:11; 15:24 and 1 Corinthians 15:12-19 underscore the centrality of miracles to the truth claims of Christianity.

First Option: Miracles Are Not Possible

Those who hold this position claim that the kinds of miracles described in the Bible cannot occur for philosophical or scientific reasons. The philosophy of naturalism asserts that the universe operates according to uniform natural causes, and that it is impossible for any force outside the universe to intervene in the cosmos. This, of course, is an antisupernatural assumption which only atheists can hold consistently.

Some philosophers have, in effect, defined miracles as events which cannot occur. David Hume (1711-1776), in his refutation of miracles, held that no amount of evidence can establish that a miracle has occurred. This, he argued, is because of the uniformity of natural law (the idea that the laws of nature are unchanging and inviolable; Hume actually denied this principle in his other works). The uniformity of natural law is in turn supported by the uniform experience of men against the occurrence of miracles. But what about the documented reports of miracles? They must be false, because they violate the uniformity of natural law! This is arguing in a circle, because it assumes the very thing that must be proven. It is not reasonable to define something as impossible and then conclude from the definition that there is no evidence for it. This is a case of determining the verdict before openly examining the evidence on its own merits.

The antisupernatural assumption must be seen for what it is: a presupposition that God either does not exist or cannot directly intrude into the historical process. This presupposition has quietly become a part of the whole scientific enterprise, so that many scientists rule out the possibility of miracles from the beginning. But when they raise this objection, they are walking on the turf of metaphysics (philosophy), not science.

The scientific method is obviously useful in gaining a great deal of knowledge, but remember that science is limited in its scope to the study of natural phenomena, especially that which is repeatable. Those who forget this fact commit one of the great mistakes of our age—the degeneration of science (a method for gaining theoretical and applied knowledge) into scientism (a naturalistic world view). Scientific laws are descriptive, not prescriptive; they describe how nature operates, but they do not cause events to happen.

Since miracles, if they occur, are empowered by something higher than nature, they must supersede the ordinary processes or laws of nature. If you took a flying leap off the edge of a sheer cliff, the phenomenon that we call the law of gravity would surely bring you to an untimely end. But if you leaped off the same cliff in a hang glider, the results would (hopefully!) be quite different. The principle of aerodynamics in this case overcomes the pull of gravity as long as the glider is in the air. In a similar way, the occurrence of a miracle means that a higher (supernatural) principle has overcome a lower (natural) principle for the duration of the miracle. To claim that miracles violate or contradict natural laws is just as improper as to say that the principle of aerodynamics violates the law of gravity.

Because miracles are accomplished by a supernatural agency, there is no natural explanation for how they happen. But our inability to explain them certainly does not mean, therefore, that they cannot take place. Scientists still cannot explain many nonmiraculous phenomena, but these phenomena occur nevertheless.

Another scientific objection to miracles is that they destroy the regularity of nature. The scientific method is built upon the assumption that we live in an orderly universe. But if divine interventions can take place at any time, anything can happen, and order is replaced by confusion. This objection is caused by a complete misunderstanding of the biblical teaching on miracles. The Bible affirms that this is an orderly universe because it has been created and sustained by an intelligent Designer. God has instituted what we call the laws of nature, but He is not bound by them. He sometimes chooses to supersede them in order to reveal something about Himself to men. But an examination of the Bible shows that these sovereign interventions or miracles are unusual, not commonplace events. In fact, a miracle by its very nature must be a unique event that stands out against the background of ordinary and regular occurrences. Thus, it is just as devastating to the concept of miracles to believe that we are surrounded by them as to say that there are no such things.

The popular song "I Believe in Miracles" illustrates the miraculous by referring to a lily pushing its way up through the stubborn sod. While the growth of a plant and the design of the human body point to the wonderful handiwork of God, it is not really correct to call these miracles. To do so would be to turn everything into miracles. This would dilute the concept of the miraculous so much that it would become useless. What we mean and what most people who raise this question mean by the term "miracle" is a phenomenon that occurs in space-time history that is so radically different from the ordinary operations of nature that its observers are justified in attributing it to the direct intervention of a supernatural agent.

Significantly, the miracles of the Bible are actually clustered around three relatively brief periods associated with the giving of new revelation by God: the times of Moses and Joshua, Elijah and Elisha, and Christ and the apostles. These miracles were irrefutable signs from God that were designed to authenticate God's revealed Word (the Law, the Prophets, and the New Testament). These three periods were separated by centuries in which only a very few miracles are recorded. The gap between Joshua and Elijah was about 540 years, and the gap between Elisha and Christ was about 830 years. The Bible is not a record of one miracle after another; its miracles were singular events that produced a profound response in those who were privileged to observe them.

In overcoming this objection to miracles, be aware of these philosophical and scientific issues, because they frequently come to the surface. But the key issue behind this whole question is whether God exists. If God created the universe, there is a supernatural dimension to reality, and this means that miracles *are* possible. If the questioner challenges the existence of God, it may be necessary to deal with this more basic issue (see Chapter 3) before moving further into the miracles question.

On the other hand, some people may prefer to delve deeper into the topic of miracles by developing the historical case for the resurrection of Jesus Christ. If a person becomes convinced of the Resurrection, he or she is certainly more likely to believe in the existence of God.

Incidentally, the idea of a miracle is relative, not absolute. To God, there are no miracles because of His omnipotence and omniscience: there is no higher power than His, and He cannot be surprised. Edwin Abbott's story, *Flatland* (1884), is often used to illustrate the difference that another dimension would make. In this book, a spherical being from a three-dimensional world visits a creature named A. Square, who lives in the two-dimensional world of Flatland. However, the concept of height is meaningless to A. Square. He can only perceive things in the two dimensions of length and width. When the spherical being intersects the plane of Flatland, A. Square is amazed to see an expanding and contracting circle (a sphere passing through a plane would appear on the plane as a circle with an increasing and decreasing diameter). The sphere also claims to be able to look inside many of the Flatland houses at once. What is normal to the sphere is considered miraculous to the dwellers of Flatland.

The idea of a higher law can also be illustrated by the story of the Martian who decided to come to our planet to observe human life. After landing his tiny spacecraft on top of a building in Chicago, the Martian began to study the effect traffic lights have on the movement of vehicles on the streets. For a solid hour he observed a consistent pattern: when the lights were green the vehicles moved; on yellow they slowed down; and on red they stopped. After formulating this as a law of traffic, he was about to leave when he suddenly spotted a vehicle with bright flashing lights on top and making loud noises. To the Martian's amazement, this vehicle actually went through a red light, violating the uniform law he had just formulated. "Aha!" he said, "there must be a higher law! When you have a flashing light and a loud sound, you can go through the crossing regardless of what color the light may be."

If a person acknowledges the existence of God, he cannot flatly deny the possibility that miracles have occurred. Now the question is not one of philosophy but of history. Miracles are possible, but is there enough evidence to show that any have happened?

Before considering this question under the Maybe option, see Chart 13 for the No option.

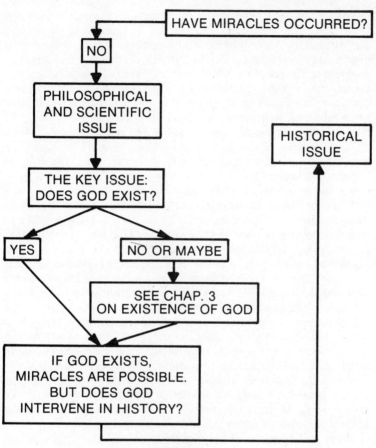

(CHART 13)

Second Option: Miracles Are Possible
But May Not Have Occurred

We have seen that the basic philosophical and scientific barrier to the miracles question is the existence of God. His existence opens up the possibility of miracles, but not all who believe in God admit that miracles have occurred.

Speculation will never settle the question of whether God has miraculously intervened in human affairs. To find an answer we must use historical evidence. The Bible takes history seriously because God used history as His means of revealing His character and redemptive program to His people. God has worked through specific people and events, and the Bible's abundant use of geographic and chronological documentation ties God's revelation to the real world. The Bible is not a fabric of myths that took place "long ago and far away." Its reliable accounts usually tell us where and when the events took place, and often relate them to the affairs of other nations. The miracles in the Bible are recorded with the same attention to historical details as the nonmiraculous events. Again, this is quite unlike the scriptures of other religions.

There are those who argue that it is beneath God's dignity to overrule the normal patterns of nature in order to reveal Himself to men. But what better way can the sovereign God who created nature use to manifest Himself to humanity? Indeed, God's clearest manifestation to mankind was His personal revelation in Jesus Christ, the greatest model of humility and servanthood the world has ever known. But this Suffering Servant accomplished more miracles than any other man before or since (cf. John 20:30; 21:25).

If we were restricted to God's general revelation of Himself in nature (natural theology), our knowledge of Him would be too limited and too speculative. It is through His special revelation in words and works that we can attain "the wisdom that leads to salvation through faith which is in Christ Jesus" (2 Tim. 3:15). The Bible claims that this special revelation includes miraculous events, and it would be improper to rule out the occurrence of miracles without an open investigation of these historical reports.

When answering this objection about God's special revelation and the question of miracles, you should limit the historical investigation to the miracles of Jesus Christ, since Christianity is built on His person and work. At this point, some people may challenge the reliability of the Gospel accounts and assert that the New Testament writers embellished the story of Jesus by adding myths about miracles He never performed. To refute this popular misunderstanding, use some of the material in chapter 6 concerning the reliability of the Bible. There was not enough time between the life of Christ and the written Gospels to allow for the evolution of this mythological Christ, and there were too many eyewitnesses who would have vehemently refuted such a distortion.

The four Gospels record 35 of the many miracles that Christ performed in His brief public ministry. In these miracles, He demonstrated His authority over nature, disease, demons, and death. They always had a redemptive purpose and were never done to dazzle people or ostentatiously display His supernatural powers. They were, in fact, accomplished with great restraint, not pride, and the Gospel accounts tend to understate rather than overstate them. The miracles of Christ were done publicly, sometimes before thousands of eyewitnesses. It is also significant that many of these eyewitnesses were hostile to Christ, including the Pharisees, Sadducees, and Herodians. None of Christ's critics ever denied that He performed these miracles. They could only challenge the source of power that He used (cf. Matt. 12:24) and His personal authority to do them (cf. Matt. 21:23). This is why Peter could boldly refer in his Acts 2 sermon on the day of Pentecost to "Jesus the Nazarene, a man attested to you by God with miracles and wonders and signs which God performed through Him in your midst (Acts 2:22).

The miracles of Christ clearly set Him apart from the founders and leaders of other world religions. Because of His uniqueness, attempts have been made to discredit His miracles by offering natural explanations for His supernatural accomplishments. For example, He didn't actually walk on the water of the Sea of Galilee—He was really walking on a sandbar that was just below the water. Or, He didn't feed the multitudes by multiplying the five loaves and two fish—when He shared the lad's lunch, the people were fed by following this example of sharing their food with one another. Of course, explanations such as these can be created only by doing a severe injustice to the text. Not only are the passages distorted, but the people themselves would have to be dolts to accept these things as miracles. The latter is precisely what is implied by some critics who are guilty of what C. S. Lewis called "chronological snobbery." This is the arrogant assumption that people in previous ages were so credulous that they could be duped into thinking that practically anything was a miracle.

It is easy to visualize an updated version of Mark Twain's *A Connecticut Yankee in King Arthur's Court.* How would people in the Dark Ages react if you could demonstrate a digital watch or a battery-powered calculator? They might conclude that these things must be divine or demonic, but this is not a fair analogy. How would *you* react if someone walked up to your boat in the middle of a lake or instantly gave sight to someone in your family who was born blind? First-century Palestine was a part of the Roman Empire, and its inhabitants were civilized people. They knew just as well as we do that there are no naturalistic explanations for such events. Many who were skeptical were forced by the evidence to admit against their bias that these things took place (cf. John 20:24-29).

Of all His miracles, Christ singled out one as the greatest sign to unbelievers: "the sign of Jonah the prophet" (the Resurrection; Matt. 12:39-40). The historical evidence for the Resurrection is very strong, and because of its significant personal implications, this is the miracle to use when answering the question, "Why believe in miracles?" If the abundant evidence convinces a person that the Resurrection took place, the miracles question must be answered in the affirmative. See the appendix to this chapter for a method, along with a flow chart, of presenting the case for the Resurrection.

It is better to use the miracles of Christ and the Resurrection in particular to answer this question than to appeal to contemporary examples. The Bible needs to be presented as the believer's final authority for truth. (The Maybe option to the miracles question is diagramed in Chart 14.)

Third Option: Miracles Have Occurred

Even if a person admits that the Resurrection and other miraculous events in the Bible took place, this is not enough. Many believe these things and still refuse to place their trust in Christ. The miracles in the Bible were signs that authenticated God's message and messengers, but those who saw them didn't always respond with faith.

The Scriptures make it clear that the heart of an unregenerate person is at enmity with God and refuses to bow to His revelation and authority. This is why the Council of Sanhedrin sought to suppress the message about the resurrected Christ even though they could not deny the Resurrection or Peter's healing of the man who had been lame from birth (Acts 4:16-17; cf. Luke 16:31; John 12:10-11). Only the Holy Spirit's work of convicting unbelievers of "sin, and righteousness, and judgment" (John 16:8) can break through the spiritual blindness of non-Christians.

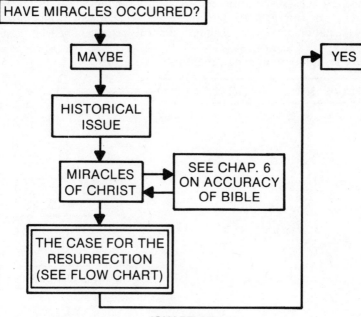

(CHART 14)

Some object that God's revelation is too remote. If He wants people to believe, He should reveal Himself in a more direct way. In effect, the objector wants God to clobber him into the kingdom by forcing him to believe. What would it take—a cloud formation spelling out John 3:16? A glowing angel hovering above his bed at 3:00 A.M.? Perhaps a fulfillment of Philip's modest request would do: "Lord, show us the Father, and it is enough for us" (John 14:8). God, however, has already done more than enough. When Jesus Christ returns to the earth, He will not come to offer salvation but to judge those who have already rejected God's offer of salvation through faith in His finished work.

Miracles cannot create faith, but they can be used by the Holy Spirit as catalysts to faith, especially when a person begins to consider the claims and credentials of Christ (see Chapter 8). Christ's miracles (especially the Resurrection) demonstrate the validity of His claims, and if His claims are true, they have profound implications for the eternal destiny of every human being. This naturally leads into a presentation of the Gospel and the biblical meaning of belief in Jesus Christ (see Chapter 13).

The third option to the question about miracles is seen in Chart 15.

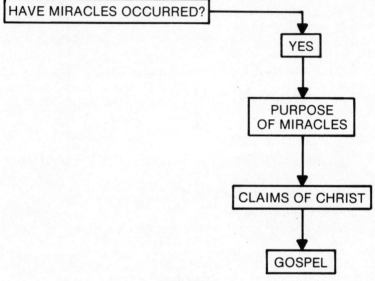

(CHART 15)

Summary and Flow Chart

Those who object to the possibility of miracles usually assume that the natural laws of the universe cannot be overruled by some outside force; it is a closed system. This antisupernatural assumption has profoundly influenced many scientists who argue that a universe open to miracles would not be orderly. But scientific inquiry is not threatened by the occurrence of miracles, because they are by definition unusual events that involve a very brief suspension of the normal processes of nature by a higher power. The real issue behind this question is whether God exists. If He does, miracles are possible. How can we know whether God has chosen to intervene in His creation through miraculous works? To answer this we must turn

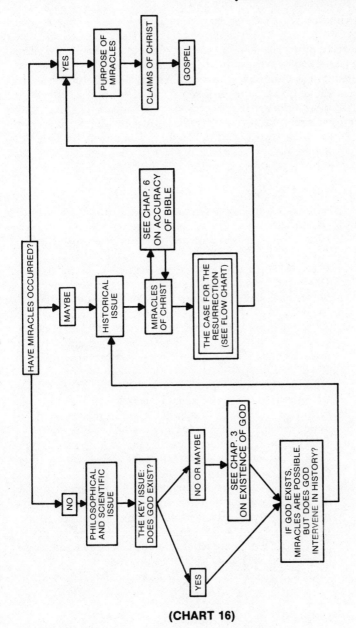

(CHART 16)

from philosophy to history. According to the Bible, God has chosen to reveal Himself in historical ways, and these include divinely empowered miracles. The miracles of Christ can be subjected to historical scrutiny because of the reliability of the New Testament documents. The clearest sign to unbelievers is His resurrection, and a presentation of the case for the Resurrection is the best way to affirm that miracles have occurred. But belief in the miracles of Christ is no guarantee of saving faith. Many have acknowledged the Resurrection without receiving Christ as their Saviour. The unbeliever needs to consider the implications of the claims and credentials of Christ for his life and respond to the convicting work of the Holy Spirit.

Supplemental Reading

(1) William Lane Craig, *The Son Rises: Historical Evidence for the Resurrection of Jesus Christ* (Moody). A new summary of the best evidence for the bodily resurrection of Christ.

(2) Gary R. Habermas, *The Resurrection of Jesus* (Baker). Chapter 1 offers a concise case for the Resurrection. Habermas relates the Resurrection to the existence of God, the deity of Christ, inspiration of Scripture, and salvation.

(3) Arlie J. Hoover, *The Case for Christian Theism* (Baker). Chapters 11 and 12 discuss miracles in general and the miracles of Christ. Chapter 16 presents the evidence for the Resurrection of Christ.

(4) Gordon R. Lewis, *Judge for Yourself* (InterVarsity Press). Chapter 4 develops the issue of miracles.

(5) C. S. Lewis, *Miracles* (Macmillan). A fine refutation of the philosophical objections to miracles.

(6) Josh McDowell, *Evidence that Demands a Verdict* (Here's Life). Chapter 10 is a good compilation of quotes that argue for the historical resurrection.

(7) Josh McDowell, *The Resurrection Factor* (Here's Life). A thorough presentation of the evidences for Christ's resurrection that systematically refutes the objections of critics.

(8) Frank Morison, *Who Moved the Stone?* (InterVarsity Press). A classic treatment of the Resurrection written by a lawyer who originally set out to disprove it.

(9) Merrill C. Tenney, *The Reality of the Resurrection*

(Moody). A detailed development of the historical background and scriptural accounts of the Resurrection.

Appendix on the Resurrection

The New Testament makes it clear that the bodily resurrection of Jesus Christ is one of the pillars that supports the Christian faith. Paul told the Corinthians: "If Christ has not been raised, your faith is worthless; you are still in your sins. Then those also who have fallen asleep in Christ have perished. If we have hoped in Christ in this life only, we are of all men most to be pitied" (1 Cor. 15:17-19). The preaching of the apostles in Acts revolved around the hub of the historical resurrection (e.g., Acts 1:22; 2:24-32; 3:15; 4:10; 10:40-41; 13:30-37; 17:31; 26:6-8, 23). Without the resurrection of Christ, Christianity would be unable to withstand critical attacks.

A number of thinkers who sought to disprove the Resurrection and thus invalidate Christianity found themselves confronted instead by such a weight of evidence in favor of the Resurrection that it forced them to bend their knees before the living Christ. A number of years ago, attorney Frank Morison planned to write a book that would lay the myth of the Resurrection to rest. But his book, *Who Moved the Stone?* did precisely the opposite, and Morison was converted to Christianity by the historical evidence for the empty tomb.

General Lew Wallace decided to create an historical novel about a Jewish contemporary of Jesus. Something quite unexpected took place, however, as he researched the background for the book. The historical evidence for the Resurrection overwhelmed him, and he wrote *Ben Hur* as a new believer in Christ.

Two relatively recent examples are C. S. Lewis and Malcolm Muggeridge. Lewis records his reluctant trek from atheism to Christianity in his autobiography, *Surprised by Joy.* He did not want to meet Christ, but the evidence brought him "kicking and screaming" into the kingdom. Muggeridge, a former editor of *Punch* magazine and a provoking analyst of modern culture, is a recent convert to Christianity. His journey from skepticism is traced in *Jesus Rediscovered* and *Chronicles of Wasted Time.*

Historical Facts

The facts that so profoundly affected these men are well grounded in historical and critical procedures. Today the consensus of scholarship acknowledges the historicity of these facts, even though scholars do not agree on the inspiration of Scripture or the interpretation of this historical data.

We will list eight of these facts. The first three relate to *preresurrection* events:

(1) Jesus suffered death by crucifixion. He endured six trials (three religious and three civil) that stretched through the night and into the morning. As a result, men cruelly beat Him about the face and body, plucked out His beard, jammed a crown of thorns into His scalp, and scourged Him by many lashes from the mutilating Roman whips. After His tormentors forced Jesus to carry the heavy crossbar for His crucifixion on His bleeding back, they drove iron nails through His hands and feet to secure Him to the cross. After His death, one of the executioners thrust a spear into His side, and "blood and water" immediately issued forth. Then the centurion pronounced Jesus dead (Mark 15:44-45).

(2) Friends placed Jesus' body in a securely guarded tomb. Joseph of Arimathea's tomb was hewn out of solid rock and had a single entrance that was closed off by rolling an "extremely large" (Mark 16:4) stone in front of it. The stone fit into a groove and would have to be rolled up an incline by several men in order to gain access to the tomb. Friends bound Jesus' body in linen wrappings along with about 100 pounds of spices (John 20:39-40), and Pilate ordered a guard of soldiers (probably Roman) stationed in front of the tomb when the stone was put in place (Matt. 27:65-66). A Roman seal on the stone certified that the body was inside and that no one had tampered with the tomb.

(3) The disciples were clearly discouraged because of the Crucifixion and entertained no hope that Jesus would rise from the dead. In spite of Jesus' repeated predictions of His resurrection, none of His followers expected His resurrection (see Luke 24).

The remaining five historical facts relate to *postresurrection* events:

(4) Jesus' friend Mary Magdalene and other followers found the tomb empty on the third day. This fact was disputed in the past, but recent studies even by critical theologians have led to a growing scholarly consensus that the tomb was indeed empty. This was clearly admitted even by Jesus' enemies, because the chief priests and elders bribed the guard to say that the body was stolen by His disciples

(Matt. 28:11-15). Certainly if the tomb were still occupied when the word about His resurrection began to spread, the authorities would have exhumed the body and put it on public display to quell the insidious rumors. But no body was ever produced and the empty tomb was never denied.

(5) The Roman seal was broken and the large stone was moved away from the sepulcher.

(6) The guard left the empty tomb and reported what had happened to the chief priests. They were given a large bribe and promised protection from punishment by Pilate who could have had them executed for their failure.

(7) The graveclothes of Jesus were found empty yet undisturbed (John 20:3-8).

(8) The followers of Jesus reported that Jesus appeared to them in bodily form on several occasions. These were eyewitness accounts, and they involved a variety of circumstances (e.g., indoors and outdoors) and people. On one occasion, Jesus appeared to more than 500 people at once (1 Cor. 15:6). In these appearances, Christ stressed that He was in a real body and offered ample demonstration of this truth. The first witnesses were women, and it is unlikely that a fabricated account would have included this since the Jewish courts regarded the testimony of women as unreliable. Jesus also appeared to His brother James and later to Paul. In every case, the lives of these witnesses were radically transformed, and this is especially difficult to explain in the case of Paul apart from the Resurrection.

These facts cannot be ignored by historians and theologians, but they can and have been interpreted in various ways to avoid the conclusion that Jesus rose from the dead. Several naturalistic theories regarding the tomb and the appearances have been proposed, but all of these fail to explain the historical data. Furthermore, there is a quantity of circumstantial evidence that supplements this data and makes the case for the Resurrection even stronger.

Explanations Regarding the Tomb

The tomb of Jesus was either occupied or empty on the first day of the week. We will first consider four theories that claim that the tomb was still occupied. Then we will examine four naturalistic theories that attempt to explain why the tomb was empty.

The first option is that the tomb was still *occupied:*

(1) The location of the tomb was unknown. This theory is completely unacceptable because all four Gospels state that Joseph of Arimathea obtained permission from Pilate to bury the body of Jesus in his newly hewn tomb near the crucifixion site. Certainly he knew the location of his own private garden tomb. The accounts also make it clear that the women and disciples had no trouble finding the tomb, and the guard certainly knew the location as well. A variation of this theory holds that Jesus' body was thrown into a common pit for the executed. This view can only be maintained by an outright denial of all four burial accounts, and there is not a shred of evidence for doing so.

(2) The women and disciples went to the wrong tomb. This theory eliminates the "He has risen" of Mark 16:6, arguing that the young man's statement to the women was simply, "He is not here; behold, here is the place where they laid Him." He was telling them that they had the wrong tomb, but the women misunderstood. There is no textual basis for changing this verse, and to be true, this theory would have to distort many other verses as well. It also requires the absurd conclusion that Peter and John, and eventually Joseph of Arimathea, the guards, and the Jewish and Roman authorities *all* went to the wrong tomb, and that the correct tomb was never found.

(3) Jesus was resurrected spiritually, not bodily. This "pious" compromise rejects the physical resurrection of Jesus but holds that He is alive. His appearances to the disciples were genuine, but they misinterpreted the nature of His resurrection. Like the other theories, this one does a severe injustice to the historical accounts. In the postresurrection narratives, Jesus placed special emphasis on the fact that His body was resurrected: "See My hands and My feet, that it is I Myself; touch Me and see, for a spirit does not have flesh and bones as you see that I have" (Luke 24:39). The disciples took hold of His feet (Matt. 28:9), Mary clung to Him (John 20:17), and He ate a piece of broiled fish before the disciples (Luke 24:42-43). Jesus stressed His physical resurrection because a mere spiritual resurrection (with His body rotting in the tomb) would have been unacceptable to the Jews; first-century Judaism correctly awaited the restoration of the whole person, including the body.

(4) A twin brother or someone who looked like Jesus was crucified and buried in His place. This desperate theory does not have a bit of evidence to support it and contradicts many clear passages. For

example, Jesus bore the marks of His crucifixion and spear wound on His resurrection body (see John 20:24-28) and physically ascended into heaven in the sight of the disciples (Acts 1:9).

The remaining option is that the tomb was *empty:*

(1) One or more of Jesus' friends stole His body. This was the original explanation for the empty tomb (see Matt. 28:11-15); the soldiers were bribed by the chief priests and elders to lie and say that the disciples stole the body while they were asleep. Of course, if they were sleeping, how could they know that the disciples were responsible? This would also require the entire guard to be asleep at the same time, a circumstance made even more unlikely by the fact that their lives were on the line if the body was stolen. Furthermore, the noise involved in rolling the huge stone away from the entire sepulcher would surely have aroused some of the soldiers from their slumber. In addition to these problems, neither Joseph of Arimathea nor the disciples would have had any real motive to steal the body. They did not expect the Resurrection to take place and had nothing to gain and everything to lose by perpetrating a deliberate fraud. The disciples endured great suffering because of their testimony about the resurrected Lord, most to the point of death. Such behavior would have been absurd if they knew it was all a lie. This kind of deception is also inconsistent with the high moral character exhibited in their New Testament epistles. Finally, how would this frightened band of men be able to overcome an armed guard of professional soldiers?

(2) The enemies of Jesus stole the body. This theory is also plagued by the problem of motive: why would the Jewish or Roman authorities want to steal the body when this is precisely the thing they sought to avoid? Even if they did remove the body for security purposes, they would have made such a claim and displayed the body, if necessary, to put an end to the rumors of the Resurrection that were circulating in Jerusalem. The complete silence on the part of the Jewish and Roman authorities loudly proclaimed their acknowledgment that the body was inexplicably gone.

(3) Jesus "swooned" on the cross and appeared to be dead. He was resuscitated by the cool air of the tomb, and His disciples were convinced He rose from the dead. This eighteenth-century rationalistic theory, when analyzed, requires as great a miracle as the Resurrection itself. It means that Jesus endured the beatings at His trials, the crown of thorns, the terrible scourging, the crucifixion,

and even the spear thrust in His side and somehow survived. The professional executioners were satisfied that He was dead and His body was wrapped in linen along with 100 pounds of spices. In spite of great loss of blood and many hours in the cold tomb without food, water, or assistance, He revived. Then He managed to escape from the graveclothes and spices and replace them neatly in the tomb; He rolled the huge stone up an incline away from the opening, overcame the armed guards, walked miles on pierced feet, and convinced His disciples that He had conquered death as the resurrected Author of life. This ludicrous theory would also have us believe that Jesus lived on after all this and died a natural death in obscurity.

(4) Jesus wanted to deceive His disciples into thinking He was the Messiah by engineering His fulfillment of the Old Testament messianic passages. He plotted with Joseph of Arimathea to receive a drug during His crucifixion that would make Him appear to be dead. Joseph was then to place Jesus in his tomb and revive Him so that the disciples would believe He had been resurrected. But the Roman spear changed these plans and Jesus lived only briefly after being revived. Joseph removed the body, and when a certain "young man" appeared a few times to the confused disciples, they thought he was Jesus. This fanciful scenario appears in *The Passover Plot,* the brainchild of Hugh Schoenfield. It requires at least as great a distortion of the historical accounts as the previous theories. Schoenfield simply rejects the many passages that disprove his theory and builds on a few verses taken completely out of context. This antiresurrection theory is totally bereft of evidence, and it makes Jesus a malicious deceiver and the disciples a band of gullible fools.

None of these theories even comes close to accounting for the historical facts associated with the empty tomb, the appearances of the resurrected Christ, and the radical changes in the lives of the disciples. They distort the clear evidence without any basis and require more faith to believe than the Resurrection itself. It is ironic that the chief priests and the Pharisees made such an effort to have the tomb secured, because had they not done so, the case for the Resurrection would not have been as strong.

Explanations of the Appearances

(1) The disciples all lied about seeing the resurrected Jesus. The first problem with this view is that it contradicts the historical accounts. It

also means that *all* of the disciples who claimed to have seen the Lord (including the 500 people mentioned by Paul) were liars. To make matters worse, these people had nothing to gain by perpetuating such a falsehood, and many of them suffered for this testimony, even to the point of violent deaths. Would this many people willingly give up their lives for the sake of a fraud?

(2) The postresurrection appearances of Christ were merely hallucinations in the minds of the disciples. There are a number of reasons why the hallucination theory does not fit the facts: (a) Hallucinations are private, not publicly shared experiences. But according to the accounts, Jesus appeared several times to groups of people including a crowd of 500. (b) Hallucinations are generally restricted to favorable places and times of day, but Christ appeared in a variety of locations and times. There was no pattern in His appearances. (c) Only certain kinds of people (e.g., people with schizoid tendencies, ascetics, those who use hallucinogenic drugs) are subject to hallucinatory experiences, but the appearances of Christ involved a great range of personalities. (d) After Christ appeared to people over a 40-day period, His appearances suddenly ceased. Hallucinations, on the other hand, generally recur over a long period of time and do not abruptly stop. (e) Hallucinations are stimulated by expectation, but the disciples had no hope at all of Christ's resurrection. They were quite skeptical about the earliest reports. (f) The disciples touched, talked, and ate with the Lord at various times, and this certainly cannot be said to be characteristic of hallucinations.

(3) The whole story of the resurrected Jesus, including the appearances, is simply an elaborate legend created by the early church. To answer this objection, it may be necessary to look at the question concerning the reliability of the Bible (see Chapter 6). These accounts were backed up by eyewitness testimonies and widely circulated without being challenged by the friends or enemies of Jesus. Peter firmly declared, "We did not follow cleverly devised tales when we made known to you the power and coming of our Lord Jesus Christ, but we were eyewitnesses of His majesty" (2 Peter 1:16). The dating of the New Testament documents also precludes the development of such a legend because there was not enough time. With every passing year, additional archaeological discoveries continue to vindicate the historical reliability of the Scriptures.

Circumstantial Evidence

(1) Christ predicted His own resurrection on the third day and announced that this would be the most significant sign for the affirmation of His truth claims. The Lord demonstrated His foreknowledge of this crucial event several times (e.g., Matt. 12:38-40; Mark 8:31; 9:31; 10:33-34; John 2:18-22).

(2) The silence of the Jewish leaders about the Resurrection eloquently testified that they knew these things were undeniable. They certainly would have offered a refutation of this Christian claim if there had been any basis for doing so.

(3) Before the Resurrection, the disciples were fearful men whose faith was weak and all abandoned Jesus after His arrest. But by the Day of Pentecost seven weeks later, they were boldly proclaiming Christ to the multitudes in Jerusalem. This transformation was complete, permanent, and unanimous. All of them suffered for the sake of the message of the resurrected Lord, and almost all died as martyrs. It is clear that they were totally convinced of the truth of the Resurrection, and they were certainly in a position to know whether the Resurrection had indeed taken place.

(4) The success of the early Christian church in spite of fierce opposition is another evidence for the Resurrection. The church began right in Jerusalem, the city of the empty tomb, and the apostles' preaching centered on the resurrected Saviour. Without the Resurrection, the church would not have come into existence.

(5) The shift from Saturday to Sunday as the day of worship for the early Jewish Christians (cf. Acts 20:7; 1 Cor. 16:1-2) was a radical act that would never have taken place if Christ had not been raised on the first day of the week (Matt. 28:1; Luke 24:1).

(6) The sacraments of baptism and communion are both related to the Resurrection, and would have been senseless in the early church apart from the historical reality of the Resurrection.

(7) The complete disregard for the tomb of Jesus by the first-century church also illustrates that these Christians knew they were serving the resurrected Lord.

(8) The conversions of James and Paul offer significant circumstantial evidence for the Resurrection. James was opposed to the claims of his half brother Jesus (John 7:5), but a transformation took place after the risen Jesus appeared to him (1 Cor. 15:7). He became the leader of the Jerusalem church and called himself a "bond-servant

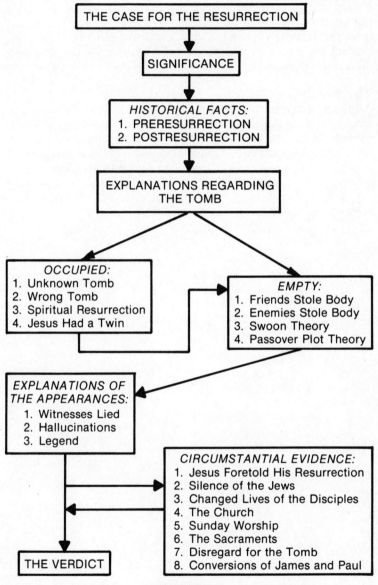

(CHART 17)

of God and of the Lord Jesus Christ" (James 1:1). The incredible change in the zealous young Pharisee, Saul, is also inexplicable apart from the Resurrection. Saul, the fierce persecutor of Christians, suddenly became Paul, the persecuted Christian. He was never the same after he beheld the glory of Christ on the road to Damascus.

The Verdict

All the attempts to find naturalistic explanations for the historical facts related to the Resurrection have failed. The direct evidence concerning the tomb and the appearances, combined with the circumstantial evidences establishes beyond a reasonable doubt the bodily resurrection of Jesus Christ. He conquered the grave, and He offers resurrection life to those who place their trust in Him.

Chart 17 plugs into the "Have Miracles Occurred?" flow chart presented earlier in this chapter.

5

Isn't Christianity Just a Psychological Crutch?

Often-Asked Questions:

Isn't Christianity, like all religions, just a crutch for emotionally weak people?

Don't people just create God in order to cope with the future?

Why should it matter what you believe as long as you have a sincere faith?

If you were raised to believe in God, can you ever deny that preconditioning?

What if I don't need religion?

Two Options

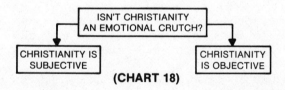

(CHART 18)

To answer this question, we must first understand the definition of the word *psychological*. It has been defined in the dictionary as "existing in the mind," or "reality as it is perceived." If an experience is merely psychological, then it must be totally subjective, without any objective data to substantiate a conclusion.

Either Christianity is a subjective experience that has no objective reality, or it is an experience that has an objective basis (see Chart 18). Before examining these two options, we should make it clear that a position is not rendered false just because it is completely subjective. This just removes it from the sphere of investigation. If Christianity can be relegated to the state of total subjectivity, we will be hard pressed to prove the validity of our claims. Remember, though, that many critics have found the corner of subjectivity a comfortable one into which they can sweep opposing views when faced with an uncomfortable decision.

First Option: Christianity Is Subjective

For centuries, religion in general and Christianity in particular have been categorized as emotional crutches. The word *crutch* has negative connotations when applied to religion. A crutch assumes: (1) the presence of a problem or need and (2) the supply of aid or assistance. The aid and assistance available in a crutch always leaves something to be desired. A crutch conjures up the notion of a clumsy device to help a person lurch through life. It is a help, not a solution to the problem. According to this view, a religious person operates strictly from emotion to meet his needs and overcome his weaknesses. The major skeptics of religion, such as Sartre, Russell, Marx, and Freud, have portrayed religion as something for the emotionally weak, for those who can't cope with the future on their own. Marx saw the problem as economic; religion is the carrot on a stick used by the upper classes to keep the lower classes from revolting. The masses were kept in tow with the promise of a better existence in the next life if they persevered now. Freud and others related religion to the fear that comes from contending with natural forces. According to Freud, man invented God to help him deal with the dangers and unknowns of life. Now that man is more sophisticated and less superstitious, there is little need for God.

We agree that religion can be a crutch. Some highly emotional and weak people seek religion because they are too insecure to face the future on their own. They invent their own gods to assist them through life's burdens and woes. Christianity is often caricatured by the media as an escape mechanism for emotionally needy people. But the fact that religion *can be* a crutch doesn't actually mean that it *always* is.

Let us now examine some psychological objections to Christianity. The first objection is *preconditioning*. Some try to invalidate the Christian's claim to be objective by stating that Christians were preconditioned to believe in Christ by their family and culture. They make two false assumptions:

(1) All Christians were raised in a Christian environment. On the contrary, a survey of Christians would indicate many came to Christianity out of religiously hostile or neutral environments.

(2) If a person is preconditioned, his position is not valid. But preconditioning does not make a position true or false. The question to be asked is, "Does my preconditioning have any objective reality?" Take this statement out of the realm of religion for a moment. Most people in America were preconditioned to believe in Santa Claus when they were young. As they matured, they understood that Santa Claus was really their parents. Their preconditioning was false because the object was false. But most people were also preconditioned when they were young to believe that fire is extremely hot, and as they matured, their experience confirmed their preconditioning. Don't allow a person to fall into the trap of rejecting Christianity just because he was preconditioned to believe it as a child. Preconditioning does not validate or invalidate a position. An investigation of the validity of Christianity's claims should lead to a search for some kind of objective basis.

Critics may attack Christianity's claim to be objective by raising a second objection: *belief and emotions do not determine truth.* They assume that Christians declare Christianity to be true on the basis of their own beliefs and emotions. But this assumption is false. Christianity is true because of Christ and who He is, and not because Christians have beliefs or emotions. One's belief in something does not make it true, and conversely, one's lack of belief does not make something false.

For example, suppose someone decides to believe that every time he throws a ball up it will come down. Does it come down because he believes it will? No, it comes down because of gravity and not because of his belief. Suppose another person no longer believed that the law of gravity existed. Would we encourage that person to leap from the tallest building in town? Obviously not, for he would plummet to earth. The law of gravity is valid on the basis of its objective criteria, and not on the basis of one's belief or lack of belief.

Or, take the case of a patient with a deadly bacterial infection. When this patient gets a dose of morphine, the symptoms of her disease are erased because of the numbing effects of the drug. The patient believes she is cured. But believing she is cured and *being* cured are two different things. Now suppose the patient receives penicillin instead of morphine. She still has her pain while being cured and thus believes that the medicine is having no effect. But her lack of belief does not alter the reality of her cure. We must remember that one's belief is only as valid as the object in which it is placed. The Christian does not attempt to validate Christianity on the basis of his subjective beliefs and emotions. Instead, he turns to the objective data regarding Christ.

The third objection raised to demonstrate that Christianity is subjective rather than objective is that *experience does not determine truth*. The assumption here is that Christians have sought to prove the truth of Christianity on the basis of their experience. This is also false. Experience or lack of it can lead a person to a conclusion, but it remains a subjective conclusion and therefore removed from the sphere of investigation. An individual's personal experience can verify truth but it doesn't prove it.

An I.Q. test will affirm that a genius is a genius, but the experience of taking the test did not make him a genius. He was a genius and the test confirmed it. A blind man may never have seen a sunset, but he should not conclude from this that sunsets don't exist.

From these objections we can conclude first that the Christian viewpoint cannot be dismissed on the basis of preconditioning. The real question should be, "Is there any objective reality to one's preconditioning?" Second, a belief or an experience does not prove a position, nor does a lack of belief or experience disprove a position. Again, the real question is whether there is any objective reality to one's belief or experience. If not, then the Christian position might be a psychological crutch.

Before delving into whether or not Christianity has any objective reality, we would do well to turn the tables on the critics of Christianity and see the psychological objections to atheism.

In *Objections Answered* (Regal), R. C. Sproul described the dilemma as follows:

> There is no dispute that man has the power of creative imagination and the capacity to turn his fantasies into

theories or full-blown religious systems. It must also be admitted that man does find in religion an important resource for comfort and consolation. That people are often attracted to religion by emotional needs is not in dispute. That religion has been used countless times in history as a tool of exploitation is not in dispute. But the same thing can be said for atheism (pp. 63-64).

It seems that on many occasions it would suit man's fancy not to have to answer to an almighty God. If there is no God, the consequences of one's actions can be minimized. Could it be that the atheist eliminates God so that his own fear of having to face such a Being can be reduced? The very character of God is disturbing to men in rebellion against Him. He is holy, unchanging, all-powerful, and all-knowing. Ability to dismiss the concept of this kind of God would alleviate a great deal of guilt in the hearts of men.

The ease with which some atheists dismiss God brings to mind a story about two frogs. The first frog noted that he had never seen anything bigger or stronger than a frog. The other frog verified this, and that gave them a sense of security. They knew that nothing could possibly overcome them, so they plopped off the pad and went about their business. Their decision, although subjective, was quite comfortable.

In the final analysis, we must ask the atheist the same questions asked of the Christian. What objective basis does the atheist have to dismiss God? Or is his position a subjective one and thus a psychological crutch? Since there is a lack of objective evidence for the atheistic position (see Chapter 3), it appears that the conclusion drawn by the atheist falls in the subjective realm.

Romans 1:18-32 gives us tremendous insight into the progression of man's sinful ways and how this affects man's view of God. Paul states that we all know that God exists both from the evidence within each of us and from the evidence in creation (1:19-20). But in the face of this holy God, men chose to repress this knowledge and became foolish rather than wise (1:21-22). After repressing their understanding of the true and holy God, man substituted the worship of the creation for the worship of the Creator (1:23-27). As a result, God gave those who forsook Him over to a depraved mind (1:28-32).

Everyone needs meaning in life. That is why every society has religious manifestations. Seeking meaning (basic questions about life) is not a sign of weakness. It is not a matter of *if* we seek meaning; only a matter of *how*. Someone once said it does not matter what we believe as long as we believe in something. But faith is only as good as the object in which it is placed.

Take, for example, the story of two men hiking in Colorado in January. When dusk came upon them quickly, their only hope for getting back to the lodge before dark was to cut across the lake. One of the men was afraid the ice would not support him and hesitated. His friend reminded him that it was the middle of January, the ice had to be at least six feet thick, and they had no reason to worry. The frightened man had little faith and so he inched his way back to the lodge. The ice supported him; his faith was small but its object was strong. Later that year the two men were again hiking and dusk came upon them suddenly. The once fearful man now suggested they cut across the lake. The first man, however, told his now brave friend that it was late May and the ice was no thicker than a quarter of an inch. But he could not be dissuaded, for his faith was great. So he ventured a few feet from shore and crashed through the ice. His faith was much stronger the second time, but the object of his faith far less sound. Our faith is only as good as its object.

Before we move on to the Christianity is objective option, see the first option in Chart 19.

Second Option: Christianity Is Objective

While probing for an objective reality, we must decide how much and what kind of proof we will need. Here we must return to chapter 3 and review the section dealing with proof.

In our quest for legal and historical proof, we turn to the object of Christianity and examine the person and work of Christ. The most critical historical event in this connection is the Resurrection. The Resurrection is the jugular vein of Christianity—if it is true, so is Christianity.

In the appendix to chapter 4, we examined in some detail the evidence and established beyond a reasonable doubt the Resurrection of Jesus Christ. The object of faith in Christianity is sound, and therefore, faith in this object is well-placed. Since Christians do not base their belief on subjective feelings but have an objective reality in which they trust, Christianity has an objective foundation and is not merely a psychological crutch.

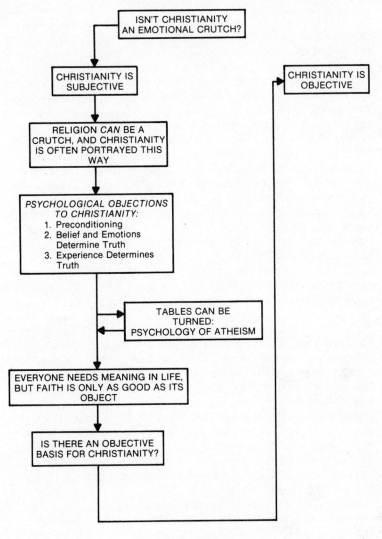

(CHART 19)

The declaration made by Christ in John 14:6, "I am the way, and the truth, and the life; no one comes to the Father but through Me," exposed the need of every man, woman, and child. If Christianity is true, we all have a real need for Christ, even though we may not feel a need. A person may have a rare disease and be in need of medical attention, even though he doesn't feel a need for it. Children have a real need for nutritional, well-balanced meals, but they may not feel they have a need.

Earlier, we said that a crutch assumes a problem or need and the supply of aid or assistance. We have already seen man's need and problem—sin which resulted in death and separation from God (Rom. 3:23; 6:23). But Christ doesn't offer a *crutch;* He gives us a *cure.* He substituted His life for ours so that we would not have to pay the penalty (Mark 10:45). This substitution was a full payment, a complete restoration. A person on a crutch is hindered and hobbles along with an artificial aid. Christians are not given a crutch for minimal assistance but are given a complete cure which provides maximal abundance.

Christians should not claim that Christianity is true because they experienced it; rather, they should say that Christianity is true and their experience confirms it. Experience plays a supportive role in substantiating the validity of Christianity. Imagine rising before dawn for a week. You stand on your back porch with a compass in hand and wait for the sun. Each morning as it rises, you position your compass and see that the sun rises in the east. Now, your getting up each morning with a compass didn't cause the sun to come up in the east. The truth is that the sun comes up in the east each morning, and your experience with the compass verified that truth.

We laid out a detailed analysis of the proofs for the Resurrection and concluded that Christianity was based on a solid foundation of objectivity rather than a shifting foundation of subjectivity. Christianity is not rejected because it has been examined and found wanting for objective truth; it is often rejected because it hasn't been examined at all.

If you are talking to an unbeliever, this is an appropriate time to focus on an explanation of the Gospel. Christ is the answer to man's problems, and we have objective verification as to His worthiness. See chapter 13 for a presentation of the Gospel and of what it means to believe. See Chart 20 for the second option to this question.

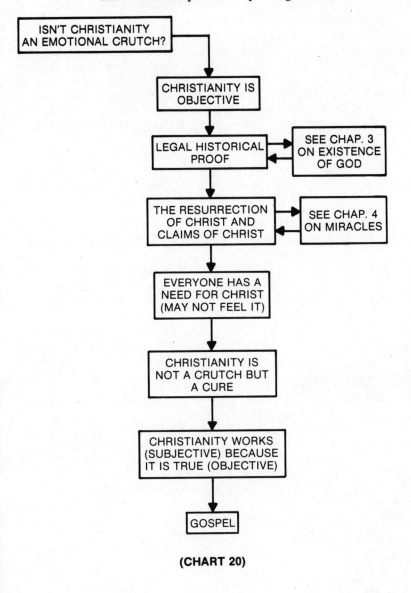

(CHART 20)

Summary and Flow Chart

Although some Christians have been influenced by preconditioning, this does not deny the reality of Christianity. The real issue is whether there is an objective reality behind it. We also argued that a belief or experience by itself is not ample reason to accept a position as objectively true. The critic of religion states that God has been created out of some emotional need. But we turned the tables and claimed that the atheist has as much to gain in meeting his own needs if God can be eliminated.

The crux of Christianity's objective reality is Christ and the Resurrection. When we examine the evidence, we must conclude that Christians rest not on a subjective mental or emotional experience but have ample objective support for their case.

Supplemental Reading

(1) David A. DeWitt, *Answering the Tough Ones* (Moody). See chapter 7.

(2) Cedric B. Johnson and H. Newton Malony, *Christian Conversion: Biblical and Psychological Perspectives* (Zondervan). An extensive examination of the factors involved in conversion.

(3) Paul E. Little, *Know Why You Believe* (Victor Books). Chapter 12 is one of the better treatments of this question.

(4) Clark H. Pinnock, *Set Forth Your Case* (Craig Press). Chapter 8 deals with "The Inadequacy of Experience Alone."

(5) R. C. Sproul, *Objections Answered* (Regal Books). Chapter 4 addresses this issue.

(6) R. C. Sproul, *If There Is a God, Why Are There Atheists?* (Bethany Fellowship). This book offers excellent insights into the other side of the coin—the psychological desire of many to do away with the existence of God.

(7) Barry Wood, *Questions Non-Christians Ask* (Revell). See chapter 3.

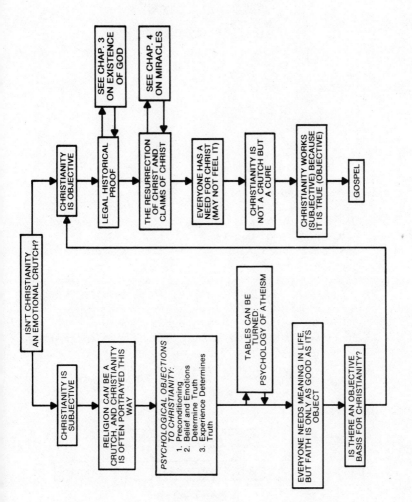

(CHART 21)

6

How Accurate
Is the Bible?

Often-Asked Questions:

Isn't the Bible full of contradictions and errors?

The Bible has been copied and translated so many times—hasn't this process led to errors?

How can you be sure that the Bible is the same now as when it was written?

Didn't the church arbitrarily decide which books should be included in the Bible and which books should be rejected?

So many people have different interpretations of the Bible—what makes you think that yours is correct?

How can you place your faith in a book that condones genocide and slavery?

Doesn't the Bible make a number of claims that are scientifically inaccurate?

Three Options

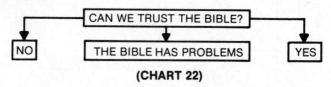

(CHART 22)

The first response to this question is a sweeping rejection of the reliability of the Bible. This attitude is almost always fostered by exposure to negative teaching about the Bible rather than firsthand investigation of its contents. The second response is a more specific problem-oriented approach that questions the veracity of the Bible because of one or more trouble spots. These include such problems as inspiration, interpretation, science and the Bible, ethics, apparent errors, canonicity, and miracles. The third response is an acknowledgment of the authority of the Bible. (See Chart 22.)

First Option: The Bible Is Not Trustworthy

This response is usually the product of false impressions that have been gained from sources other than the Bible. Most people's knowledge about the Bible is derived almost completely from second-, third-, and fourth-hand sources. It is not surprising, then, that so many people think that the Bible says, "God helps those who help themselves," or, "Cleanliness is next to godliness." Many are also convinced that the Scriptures teach that the earth is flat or that it is the center of the universe. Another common misconception is that the books of the New Testament were written centuries after the events they describe or that our earliest New Testament manuscripts go back only to the fourth or fifth centuries A.D. Also, most people have somehow been given the impression that the English Bible is a translation of a translation of a translation (etc.) of the original, and that fresh errors were introduced in each stage of the process.

College courses often undermine the authority of the Bible by falsely claiming that the Old Testament is merely a derivative of earlier Babylonian and Assyrian myths and law codes. People frequently say that the Bible is loaded with contradictions, but very few can think of any when asked. The few who can will usually mention the stock objections they were taught, like the two "contradictory" creation accounts in Genesis 1 and 2. It is a rare person who has personally examined the text to see if the alleged contradiction is really there.

As a result of all this, you may have to straighten out some of these false impressions before you can make any further progress in answering this question. You may overcome several misconceptions with a brief presentation of the case for the reliability of the biblical documents. (Note that sometimes you can use an alternate approach at this point. When someone says, "I don't believe the Bible," you can ask, "Do you understand the message of the Bible?" Many will acknowledge that they do not, and those who think they do will almost invariably present a distorted picture. After you graciously point this out, say, "I think you owe it to yourself to have a correct picture of the basic message of the Bible before you decide to accept or reject it." This can open the door to a clear presentation of the Gospel, and the discussion can go from there. This approach is only appropriate when the objection to the Bible is vague or being used as a smokescreen. If a person has honest intellectual difficulties about the Bible, give direct answers whenever possible.)

The Reliability of the Biblical Documents

This can be demonstrated by combining three lines of evidence: the bibliographic test, the internal test, and the external test. The first test examines the biblical manuscripts, the second test deals with the claims made by the biblical authors, and the third test looks to outside confirmation of biblical content.

The bibliographic test. This test examines the transmission of the text of the Old and New Testaments from the original autographs to the present day. The three aspects of this test are the quantity, quality, and time span of the manuscripts.

(1) The *quantity* of manuscripts. In the case of the Old Testament, there is a small number of Hebrew manuscripts, because the Jewish scribes ceremonially buried imperfect and worn manuscripts. Many ancient manuscripts were also lost or destroyed during Israel's turbulent history. Also, the Old Testament text was standardized by the Masoretic Jews by the sixth century A.D., and all manuscripts that deviated from the Masoretic Text were evidently eliminated. But the existing Hebrew manuscripts are supplemented by the Dead Sea Scrolls, the Septuagint (a third-century B.C. Greek translation of the Old Testament), the Samaritan Pentateuch, and the Targums (ancient paraphrases of the Old Testament), as well as the Talmud (teachings and commentaries related to the Hebrew Scriptures).

The quantity of New Testament manuscripts is unparalleled in ancient literature. There are over 5,000 Greek manuscripts, about 8,000 Latin manuscripts, and another 1,000 manuscripts in other languages (Syriac, Coptic, etc.). In addition to this extraordinary number, we have tens of thousands of citations of New Testament passages by the early church fathers. In contrast, the typical number of existing manuscript copies for any of the works of the Greek and Latin authors, such as Plato, Aristotle, Caesar, or Tacitus, ranges from one to 20.

(2) The *quality* of manuscripts. Because of the great reverence the Jewish scribes held toward the Scriptures, they exercised extreme care in making new copies of the Hebrew Bible. The entire scribal process was specified in meticulous detail to minimize the possibility of even the slightest error. The number of letters, words, and lines were counted, and the middle letters of the Pentateuch and the Old Testament were determined. If a single mistake was discovered, the entire manuscript would be destroyed.

As a result of this extreme care, the quality of the manuscripts of the Hebrew Bible surpasses all other ancient manuscripts. The 1947 discovery of the Dead Sea Scrolls provided a significant check on this, because these Hebrew scrolls antedate the earliest Masoretic Old Testament manuscripts by about 1,000 years. But in spite of this time span, the number of variant readings between the Dead Sea Scrolls and the Masoretic Text is quite small, and most of these are variations in spelling and style.

While the quality of the Old Testament manuscripts is excellent, that of the New Testament is very good—considerably better than the manuscript quality of other ancient documents. Because of the thousands of New Testament manuscripts, there are many variant readings, but these variants are actually used by scholars to reconstruct the original readings by determining which variant best explains the others in any given passage. Some of these variant readings crept into the manuscripts because of visual errors in copying or because of auditory errors when a group of scribes copied manuscripts that were read aloud. Other errors resulted from faulty writing, memory, and judgment, and still others from well-meaning scribes who thought they were correcting the text. Nevertheless, only a small number of these differences affect the sense of the passages, and only a fraction of these have any real consequences. Furthermore, *no* variant readings are significant enough to call into question any of the doctrines of the New Testament. The New Testament can be regarded as 99.5 percent pure, and the correct readings for the remaining 0.5 percent can often be ascertained with a fair degree of probability by the practice of textual criticism.

(3) The *time span* of manuscripts. Apart from some fragments, the

earliest Masoretic manuscript of the Old Testament is dated at A.D. 895. This is due to the systematic destruction of worn manuscripts by the Masoretic scribes. However, the discovery of the Dead Sea Scrolls dating from 200 B.C. to A.D. 68 drastically reduced the time span from the writing of the Old Testament books to our earliest copies of them.

The time span of the New Testament manuscripts is exceptional. The manuscripts written on papyrus came from the second and third centuries A.D. The John Rylands Fragment (P52) of the Gospel of John is dated at A.D. 117-38, only a few decades after the Gospel was written. The Bodmer Papyri are dated from A.D. 175-225, and the Chester Beatty Papyri date from about A.D. 250. The time span for most of the New Testament is less than 200 years (and some books are within 100 years) from the date of authorship to the date of our earliest manuscripts. This can be sharply contrasted with the average gap of over 1,000 years between the composition and the earliest copy of the writings of other ancient authors.

To summarize the bibliographic test, the Old and New Testaments enjoy far greater manuscript attestation in terms of quantity, quality, and time span than any other ancient documents. It is especially interesting to make specific comparisons between the New Testament and other writings (see Chart 23).

AUTHOR	DATE WRITTEN	EARLIEST COPY	TIME SPAN	NUMBER OF COPIES	ACCURACY
Homer	ca. 850 B.C.	————	——————	643	95%
Herodotus	ca. 450 B.C.	ca. A.D. 900	About 1,350 years	8	Not enough copies to reconstruct the original.
Euripedes	ca. 440 B.C.	ca. A.D. 1100	About 1,500 years	9	
Thucydides	ca. 420 B.C.	ca. A.D. 900	About 1,300 years	8	
Plato	ca. 380 B.C.	ca. A.D. 900	About 1,300 years	7	
Aristotle	ca. 350 B.C.	ca. A.D. 1100	About 1,400 years	5	
Caesar	ca. 60 B.C.	ca. A.D. 900	About 950 years	10	
Catullus	ca. 50 B.C.	ca. A.D. 1500	About 1,600 years	3	
Livy	ca. 10 B.C.	——————	——————	20	
Tacitus	ca. A.D. 100	ca. A.D. 1100	About 1,000 years	20	
New Testament	ca. A.D. 60	ca. A.D. 130	About 100 years	About 14,000	99.5%

(CHART 23)

The internal test. The second test of the reliability of the biblical documents asks, "What claims does the Bible make about itself?"

This may appear to be circular reasoning. It sounds like we are using the testimony of the Bible to prove that the Bible is true. But we are really examining the truth claims of the various authors of the Bible and allowing them to speak for themselves. (Remember that the Bible is not one book but many books woven together.) This provides significant evidence that must not be ignored.

A number of biblical authors claim that their accounts are primary, not secondary. That is, the bulk of the Bible was written by men who were eyewitnesses of the events they recorded. John wrote in his Gospel, "And he who has seen has borne witness, and his witness is true; and he knows that he is telling the truth, so that you also may believe" (John 19:35, see 21:24). In his first epistle, John wrote, "What was from the beginning, what we have heard, what we have seen with our eyes, what we beheld and our hands handled concerning the Word of life . . . what we have seen and heard we proclaim to you also" (1 John 1:1, 3). Peter makes the same point abundantly clear: "For we did not follow cleverly devised tales when we made known to you the power and coming of our Lord Jesus Christ, but we were eyewitnesses of His majesty" (2 Peter 1:16; also see Acts 2:22; 1 Peter 5:1).

The independent eyewitness accounts in the New Testament of the life, death, and resurrection of Christ were written by men who were intimately acquainted with Jesus Christ. Their Gospels and epistles reveal their integrity and complete commitment to the truth, and they maintained their testimony even through persecution and martyrdom. All the evidence inside and outside the New Testament runs contrary to the claim made by form criticism that the early church distorted the life and teachings of Christ. Most of the New Testament was written between A.D. 47 and 70, and all of it was complete before the end of the first century. There simply was not enough time for myths about Christ to be created and propagated. And the multitudes of eyewitnesses who were alive when the New Testament books began to be circulated would have challenged blatant historical fabrications about the life of Christ. The Bible places great stress on accurate historical details, and this is especially obvious in the Gospel of Luke and the Book of Acts, Luke's two-part masterpiece (see his prologue in Luke 1:1-4).

The external test. Because the Scriptures continually refer to historical events, they are verifiable; their accuracy can be checked by external evidence. Notice, for example, the chronological details in the prologue to Jeremiah (1:1-3) and in Luke 3:1-2. Ezekiel 1:2 allows us to date Ezekiel's first vision of God to the day (July 31, 592 B.C.).

The historicity of Jesus Christ is well-established by early Roman, Greek, and Jewish sources, and these extrabiblical writings affirm the major details of the New Testament portrait of the Lord. The first-century Jewish historian Flavius Josephus made specific references to John the Baptist, Jesus Christ, and James in his *Antiquities of the Jews.* In this work, Josephus gave us many background details about the Herods, the Sadducees and Pharisees, the high priests like Annas and Caiaphas, and the Roman emperors mentioned in the Gospels and Acts.

We find another early secular reference to Jesus in a letter written a little after A.D. 73 by an imprisoned Syrian named Mara Bar-Serapion. This letter to his son compares the deaths of Socrates, Pythagoras, and Christ. Other first- and second-century writers who mention Christ include the Roman historians Cornelius Tacitus (*Annals*) and Suetonius (*Life of Claudius, Lives of the Caesars*), the Roman governor Pliny the Younger (*Epistles*), and the Greek satirist Lucian (*On the Death of Peregrine*). Jesus is also mentioned a number of times in the Jewish Talmud.

The Old and New Testaments make abundant references to nations, kings, battles, cities, mountains, rivers, buildings, treaties, customs, economics, politics, dates, etc. Because the historical narratives of the Bible are so specific, many of its details are open to archeological investigation. While we cannot say that archeology *proves* the authority of the Bible, it is fair to say that archeological evidence has provided external confirmation of hundreds of biblical statements. Higher criticism in the 19th century made many damaging claims that would completely overthrow the integrity of the Bible, but the explosion of archeological knowledge in the 20th century reversed almost all of these claims. Noted archeologists such as William F. Albright, Nelson Glueck, and G. Ernest Wright developed a great respect for the historical accuracy of the Scriptures as a result of their work.

Out of the multitude of archeological discoveries related to the Bible, consider a few examples to illustrate the remarkable external substantiation of biblical claims. Excavations at Nuzi (1925-41), Mari (discovered in 1933), and Alalakh (1937-39; 1946-49) provide helpful background information that fits well with the Genesis stories of the patriarchal period. The Nuzi tablets and Mari letters illustrate the patriarchal customs in great detail, and the Ras Shamra tablets discovered in ancient Ugarit in Syria shed much light on Hebrew prose and poetry and Canaanite culture. The Ebla tablets discovered recently in northern Syria also affirm the antiquity and accuracy of the Book of Genesis.

Some scholars once claimed that the Mosaic Law could not have been written by Moses, because writing was largely unknown at that time and because the law code of the Pentateuch was too sophisticated for that period. But the codified Laws of Hammurabi (ca. 1700 B.C.), the Lipit-Ishtar code (ca. 1860 B.C.), the Laws of Eshnunna (ca. 1950 B.C.), and the even earlier Ur-Nammu code have refuted these claims.

The biblical description of the Hittite Empire was confirmed contrary to the challenges of the critics when the Hittite capital was discovered in 1906. This discovery also revealed that the Book of Deuteronomy, a covenant renewal document, actually used the six-part structure of the Hittite treaties between the king and his vassals.

Other excavations agree with the account in Joshua about the conquest of Canaan and shed light on the period of the Judges and the reigns of Saul and David. Excavations at Hazor, Gezer, Megiddo, and Jerusalem and Phoenician inscriptions illuminate Solomon's reign.

Archeology also provides helpful information about the period of the divided kingdom. The Moabite Stone yields information about the reign of Omri, the sixth king of Israel. The Black Obelisk of Shalmaneser III depicts how King Jehu of Israel had to submit to the Assyrian king. The Taylor Prism has an Assyrian text which describes Sennacherib's siege of Jerusalem when Hezekiah was king. The Lachish Letters refer to Nebuchadnezzar's invasion of Judah and illustrate the life and times of Jeremiah the prophet.

Archeological finds undergird the Babylonian exile and postexilic period as described in the books of Ezra, Nehemiah, Esther, Ezekiel, Daniel, Haggai, Zechariah, and Malachi. Growing archeological and linguistic evidence points to a sixth century B.C. date for the Book of Daniel in spite of critics who assign a late date to this book to make it a prophecy after the events. Some scholars questioned the accuracy of Daniel 5 which calls Belshazzar the king of Babylon. Since archeological records say that Nabonidus was king at this time and do not refer to anyone named Belshazzar, some scholars assumed that Daniel was in error. But in 1956, three stelae (inscribed stone slabs) found in Haran cleared up the problem by showing that King Nabonidus had entrusted kingship to his son Belshazzar while he went on a campaign against the invading Persians. Ezra's description of the liberation of the city of Babylon by the Persian king Cyrus and Cyrus' decree granting permission for the Jews to rebuild their temple in Jerusalem are authenticated by the discovery of the important Cyrus Cylinder.

The New Testament has also received abundant support from archeology, and many critical attacks have been reversed. Most of the geographical details associated with the life of Jesus in the Gospels have been substantiated. This includes places such as the Pool of Siloam, the Pool of Bethesda, Jacob's Well, Bethlehem, Nazareth, Cana, Capernaum, Chorazin, the residence of Pilate in Jerusalem, and "The Pavement" in John 19:13.

In the past critics tried to discredit Luke as an accurate historian, but Luke and Acts have now been substantiated by external evidence. Luke's frequent references to cities, Roman provinces, and political figures make his writings vulnerable to historical examination. For example, critics scoffed at his reference to Lysanius as the "tetrarch of Abilene" (Luke 3:1). But archeologists recently found two Greek inscriptions which prove that Lysanius was indeed the tetrarch of Abilene in A.D. 14-29. Luke's use of technical terminology like *proconsul, procurator, Asiarch, praetor,* and *politarch* has been challenged in the past, but mounting evidence has vindicated his accuracy.

Conclusion concerning reliability. The Old and New Testaments pass the bibliographic, internal, and external tests like no other ancient books. Most professional archeologists and historians acknowledge the historicity of the Bible and yet many theologians still embrace prearcheological critical theories about the Bible. The evidence strongly supports the accuracy of the Bible in relation to history and culture, but in many cases it has been overlooked or rejected because of philosophical presuppositions that run contrary to the Scriptures. This leads to a double standard: critics approach secular literature with one standard but wrongly use a different standard when they examine the Bible. Those who discard the Bible as historically untrustworthy must realize that the same standard would force them to eliminate almost all ancient literature.

We have already seen that Christ cannot be dismissed as a mythical creation of the early church. All the evidence supports the historical reliability of the Gospel accounts about Jesus. Because of this, a solid case can be built for the resurrection of Jesus (see the appendix to chapter 4). The Resurrection, in turn, authenticates Jesus' divine claims about Himself. Because Jesus is God, His testimony concerning the Scriptures is true, and He bore witness to the complete authority of the Word of God. Thus, the historical reliability of the New Testament affirms the resurrection of Christ, and the resurrected Christ affirms the divine authority of the Scriptures.

Uniqueness of the Bible

The argument for the reliability of the biblical documents demonstrates that the Bible is trustworthy. However, it is sometimes helpful to talk briefly about the uniqueness of the Bible and the beneficial effects of the Bible to strengthen the case even more.

The uniqueness of the Bible supports its claim to be the revealed Word of God. The Bible is unique in its *production*. It is a unity out of diversity, not just an anthology of stories, poetry, and letters. The Bible is a harmonious and continuous message from beginning to end, a self-consistent whole whose main theme is the person and work of Jesus Christ. The scarlet thread of redemption runs from Genesis to Revelation. But consider the incredible diversity which produced such a unity! (1) *Diversity of authors.* There were more than 40 authors who contributed to the Bible, including a king, a herdsman, a fisherman, and a tax collector. They cover the range from educated to uneducated, from rich to poor. The Bible was written in three languages on three continents under all types of conditions. (2) *Time span.* The Bible was written over a span of about 1,500 to 1,800 years. (3) *Literary form.* The Bible includes narrative history, poetry, biography, drama, exposition, letters, parables, prophecies, sermons, narrative stories, and wisdom literature. In spite of this diversity and the controversial topics addressed in the Bible, the books of the Bible can be interwoven into a composite whole. If 10 people with similar backgrounds were selected today to write independently on a few controversial topics, the composite result would probably look like a crazy quilt of contradictory concepts.

The Bible is also unique in its *preservation.* We have just seen how the quantity, quality, and time span of the biblical manuscripts set them apart from other ancient literature. The Scriptures have survived through time, persecution, and criticism. There have been numerous attempts to burn, ban, and systematically eliminate the Bible, but all have failed. Critics have often sounded its death knell, but the corpse never stays put. The Bible has been subjected to more abuse, perversion, destructive criticism, and pure hate than any other book. Yet it continues to stand the test of time while its critics are refuted and forgotten. No other book has enjoyed such popularity— the Bible has been copied and circulated more extensively than any other book in human history. It has been translated into more languages than any other literature as well (portions now exist in more than 1,700 languages).

The Bible is unique in its *proclamations.* Its prophetic character stands alone in its content, completeness, detail, and accuracy. More than one fourth of the Bible was prophetic at the time of writing. The Bible's sweeping scope is also unparalleled as it boldly moves from eternity to eternity and touches the heights of heaven and the depths of hell. It is a progressive revelation which outlines God's plan of the ages for all creatures, including men and angels. Its revelation of God as the triune, infinite, and personal God is unique, and so is its message about man (originally created perfect; the Fall; man's sinfulness) and salvation (faith in Christ, not human merit; directly confronts and solves the problem of sin; God Himself became a man and died to redeem sinners). The Bible's strong historical emphasis also sets it apart from the scriptures of other religions.

Beneficial Effects of the Bible

The *product* of the Bible is also unique. The message of the Bible has shaped the course of history, thought, and culture in a way unparalleled by any other book. Its influence on the philosophy, morality, law, politics, art, music, literature, education, and religion of Western civilization is beyond estimation. It has also had a phenomenal impact on the lives of untold millions of people through the centuries. Its redemptive message has consistently given help, joy, and meaning to everyone who has personally embraced it.

The German poet Goethe wrote, "Belief in the Bible, the fruit of deep meditation, has served me as the guide of my moral and literary life. I have found it a capital safely invested, and richly productive of interest." The great philosopher Immanuel Kant claimed, "The existence of the Bible, as a book for the people, is the greatest benefit which the human race has ever experienced. Every attempt to belittle it is a crime against humanity." And the English philosopher John Locke wrote, "It has God for its author, salvation for its end, and truth without any mixture of error for its matter."

Chart 24 sums up the basic steps in overcoming the objection that the Bible is not trustworthy.

Second Option: There Are Problems with the Bible

The first option involved an outright denial of the reliability of the Bible. This option focuses on particular problems that cause some people to question the authority of the Bible. A person may still have one or more specific intellectual problems even after he realizes the Bible is reliable. These must be cleared up before he can confidently acknowledge the authority of the Bible. Most of these obstacles fit in the following seven categories: the problem of inspiration, interpretation, science and the Bible, ethical problems in the Bible, apparent errors, canonicity, and the miracles in the Bible. It is wise to clear up these problems in the quickest way possible, because any of them could otherwise become quite involved.

The Problem of Inspiration

A person may grant the reliability of the biblical documents but balk at the idea that they are divinely inspired. The Bible's repeated claim of verbal inspiration by God does not by itself prove such inspiration any more than similar claims made by the *Koran* or the *Book of Mormon* prove the inspiration of those books. But if all other lines of evidence point consistently to the reliability of the Bible, the Bible's self-testimony of divine inspiration must be taken seriously. Similarly, if Jesus Christ fulfilled hundreds of messianic prophecies and rose from the dead, His testimony concerning Himself and the Bible cannot be lightly dismissed.

(1) *Biblical claims.* Referring to "The Law and the Prophets" (Luke 16:16), Jesus made this unqualified statement: "But it is easier for heaven and earth to pass away than for one stroke of a letter of the Law to fail" (Luke 16:17). He said that "all things which are written about Me in the Law of Moses and the Prophets and the Psalms must

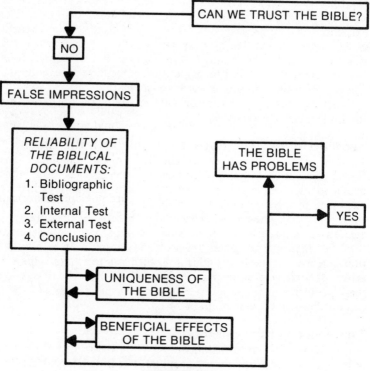

(CHART 24)

be fulfilled" (Luke 24:44), and that "the Scripture cannot be broken" (John 10:35; also see Matt. 4:4; 5:17-18; 15:4). Paul also affirmed that the Scriptures are "God-breathed" (inspired): "All Scripture is inspired by God and profitable for teaching, for reproof, for correction, for training in righteousness" (2 Tim. 3:16; also see 1 Cor. 2:13; Gal. 3:16). Peter referred to this divine-human nature of Scripture when he wrote, "No prophecy was ever made by an act of human will, but men moved by the Holy Spirit spoke from God" (2 Peter 1:21; also see 3:16).

(2) *Fulfilled prophecy.* No other book in the world contains the kind of specific prophecies found all throughout the pages of the Bible. There is no comparison, for example, between the *Oracles of*

Nostradamus and the Old Testament prophecies about Jesus Christ. Other so-called prophecies are so vague and cryptic that they could be "fulfilled" in any number of ways. But the prophecies of the Old Testament are often so detailed that their fulfillments were obvious— so clear, in fact, that many critics have attempted to assign later dates to some of these prophets (e.g., Isaiah 40—66 and Daniel) to make the prophecies come after the events. The Old Testament prophets gave both short- and long-term prophecies, so that the undisputed fulfillment of the short-term predictions would authenticate the validity of the long-term predictions which could not be verified for many years. Thus, God designed fulfilled prophecy to be an open demonstration of the divine origin of the Scriptures.

Earlier in this chapter we defended the historical trustworthiness of the biblical documents. The evidence for fulfilled prophecy will now carry us one step farther: the Scriptures are not only historically trustworthy, but they are also divinely inspired. We will focus first on messianic prophecy and then on general prophecy.

It is better to begin with *messianic prophecy* because so much of it is quite specific, and evidence shows that it was all written hundreds of years before the birth of Jesus Christ. The Old Testament was translated into Greek around 250 B.C. (the Septuagint), so it is obvious that the Hebrew Bible was written before this time. When these messianic prophecies are combined, the prophetic doorway becomes so narrow that only one person can fit through. Some 300 Old Testament predictions were literally fulfilled in the life of Jesus Christ, and these messianic predictions make no sense apart from His life. A messianic impostor might have been able to engineer the fulfillment of a few of these prophecies, but the vast majority would be beyond his reach. Jesus' sinless character, miraculous ministry, and resurrection could be matched by none other than the Messiah.

Jesus knew the Scriptures thoroughly and frequently claimed that the whole Hebrew Bible ("the Law of Moses and the Prophets and the Psalms," Luke 24:44) pointed ahead to Him. "And beginning with Moses and with all the prophets, He explained to them the things concerning Himself in all the Scriptures" (Luke 24:27; also see Matt. 5:17; 11:10; 21:42; 26:56; Luke 4:20-21; 22:37; John 5:39, 46-47; 15:25). The New Testament writers likewise claim that Jesus fulfilled the Old Testament messianic prophecies. "And according to Paul's custom, he went to them, and for three Sabbaths reasoned with them from the Scriptures, explaining and giving evidence that the Christ had to suffer and rise again from the dead, and saying, 'This Jesus whom I am proclaiming to you is the Christ'" (Acts 17:2-3; also see Acts 2:24-36; 3:18; 8:32-35; 10:43; 13:29; 1 Cor. 15:3-4; Hebrews 1:8-9, 13; 10:5-17; 1 Peter 1:10-12; 2:6-8).

The most explicit and powerful of all messianic prophecies is Isaiah 52:13—53:12, written seven centuries before the birth of Christ. This song of the Suffering Servant reveals that Messiah would suffer sinlessly (53:4-6, 9), silently (53:7), and as a substitute to bear the sins of others (53:5-6, 8, 10-12). Messiah will be subject to "scourging," "pierced through," "cut off out of the land of the living," and placed in the grave of "a rich man in His death." But after His death He will be "lifted up and greatly exalted" (52:13). This is a clear portrait of the rejection, death, burial, and resurrection of Jesus the Messiah. (Jewish scholars since the 12th century have attempted to identify the Servant of this passage with Israel, but the nation is distinguished from the Servant in 53:8, and Israel never suffered sinlessly nor silently as this Servant does.)

The following list of Old Testament predictions and New Testament fulfillments regarding the life of Christ demonstrate how thoroughly His coming was foretold: (1) *born of a woman* (Gen. 3:15; Gal. 4:4); (2) *born of a virgin* (Isa. 7:14; Matt. 1:18-25); (3) *a descendant of Abraham* (Gen. 12:1-3; 22:18; Matt. 1:1; Gal. 3:16); (4) *from the tribe of Judah* (Gen. 49:10; Luke 3:23, 33); (5) *of the house of David* (2 Sam. 7:12; Jer. 23:5; Matt. 1:1; Luke 1:32); (6) *born in Bethlehem* (Micah 5:2; Matt. 2:1; Luke 2:4-7); (7) *His way prepared by a forerunner* (Isa. 40:3-5; Mal. 3:1; Matt. 3:1-3; Luke 3:3-6); (8) *anointed by the Holy Spirit* (Isa. 11:2; Matt. 3:16-17); (9) *preaching ministry* (Isa. 61:1-3; Luke 4:17-21); (10) *speaking in parables* (Ps. 78:2-4; Matt. 13:34-35); (11) *healing ministry* (Isa. 35:5-6; Matt. 9:35); (12) *a prophet* (Deut. 18:18; John 6:14; Acts 3:20-22); (13) *a priest* (Ps. 110:4; Heb. 5:5-6); (14) *time of His appearance and death* (Dan. 9:24-27; Luke 19:44); (15) *triumphal entry* (Zech. 9:9; John 12:12-16); (16) *betrayal price* (Zech. 11:12-13; Matt. 26:15; 27:7-10); (17) *abandoned by His disciples* (Zech. 13:6-7; Matt. 26:31; Mark 14:50); (18) *silent before His accusers* (Isa. 53:7; Matt. 27:12-14); (19) *beaten and spat upon* (Isa. 50:6; Matt. 26:67); (20) *mocked* (Ps. 22:7-8; Luke 23:35); (21) *hands and feet pierced* (Ps. 22:16; John 19:16-18); (22) *crucified with transgressors* (Isa. 53:12; Mark 15:27-28); (23) *lots cast for His garments* (Ps. 22:18; John 19:23-24); (24) *cry from the cross* (Ps. 22:1; Matt. 27:46); (25) *no bones broken* (Ps. 24:20; John 19:31-36); (26) *pierced in His side* (Zech. 12:10; John 19:34, 37); (27) *buried with the rich* (Isa. 53:9; Matt. 27:57-60); (28) *resurrection and exaltation* (Ps. 16:10; Isa. 52:13; 53:10-12; Acts 2:25-32); (29) *ascension into heaven* (Ps. 68:18; Acts 1:9; Eph. 4:8); and (30) *seated at the right hand of God* (Ps. 110:1; Heb. 1:3).

Nonmessianic or *general prophecy* can also be used to illustrate the supernatural origin of the Scriptures. In many cases these prophecies are so graphic and accurate that higher criticism has assigned dates to some books and portions of books that are later than those claimed by the books themselves, because they assume that such prophecy is not possible. The accumulating evidence is generally in favor of the earlier dates, but even if we grant the later dates, many powerful examples of prediction and fulfillment in Old Testament prophecy remain.

Ezekiel's prediction of the destruction of Tyre (Ezek. 26) claims to have been given in the sixth century B.C., but higher critics date it in the fifth century B.C. According to this prophecy, Nebuchadnezzar would besiege and destroy the city (26:7-11), many nations would come against it (26:3), the ruins would be scraped from the site and thrown into the sea, leaving a bare rock (26:4, 12, 19), the site would become a place for fishermen to spread their nets (26:5, 14), and the city would never be built again (26:13-14). These specific predictions have been fulfilled in surprising detail. The ancient city of Tyre was a prominent Phoenician seaport that consisted of two parts, one on the mainland at the coast, and the other on an island about a half mile off the coast. Nebuchadnezzar besieged the mainland city for 13 years (586-573 B.C.) and finally destroyed it, but the island city remained intact. This remaining portion continued until Alexander the Great overthrew it in 332 B.C. by building a causeway from the coast to the island. To build this causeway, he literally scraped the ruins and debris from the old mainland site (26:4) and threw them "into the water" (26:12). This left the old site "a bare rock" (26:4). "Many nations" (26:3) came against the restored island city, including the Seleucids, the Ptolemies, the Romans, the Moslems, and the Crusaders. But the mainland city was never rebuilt (26:14), and today it remains a bare rock upon which fishermen spread their nets to dry (26:5, 14).

Other remarkable examples of the accuracy of Old Testament prophecies include the details about the overthrow of Nineveh (Nahum 1—3), Babylon (Isa. 13—14; Jer. 51), Ammon and Moab (Jer. 48—49; Ezek. 25), Philistia (Jer. 47; Zeph. 2), Edom (Isa. 34: Jer. 49; Ezek. 25; 35), Memphis and Thebes (Ezek. 30), and the desolation and restoration of Palestine (Lev. 26; Ezek. 36).

The biblical claims for its divine inspiration, combined with the forceful evidence of fulfilled messianic and general prophecy, make a strong case for the inspiration of Scripture, especially when these lines of evidence are built upon the case for the historical reliability of the biblical documents developed earlier in this chapter.

The Problem of Interpretation

We have often heard people say, "All these Christian denominations and organizations have their own way of interpreting the Bible. There must be thousands of different interpretations. What makes you think that yours is correct?" While it is true that Christians disagree about many issues (e.g., Genesis 1—2, war, prophetic themes), there is far wider agreement over the cardinal doctrines of Christianity than most people think. Most denominations share the foundational truths about God, man, sin, and salvation (what C. S. Lewis called "mere Christianity"). The vast majority of Christians, for example, concur with the Apostles' Creed and the Nicene Creed.

When interpretive disagreement occurs, it is usually because of faulty or inconsistent methods of interpretation (hermeneutics). For instance, some people impose their own preconceived notions upon the pages of Scripture (eisegesis) instead of allowing Scripture to speak for itself (exegesis). Apply a few simple principles of interpretation, and most difficulties disappear.

The most crucial of these principles is context; every passage should be interpreted in light of the immediate and broad context. Verses lifted out of context can be twisted to mean almost anything, but when we consider the context of the passage and the whole book, the options generally reduce to one. Another key principle is the need to interpret each passage in a plain or normal way. A text should not be understood symbolically, spiritually, or allegorically unless the context makes it clear that symbolic or parabolic speech is being used. This still allows for figures of speech such as similes and metaphors. Also, Scripture is its own best interpreter, and unclear passages on any topic should always be interpreted in the light of clear passages. These hermeneutical principles should be applied consistently throughout the Bible.

For many people, the real problem is not so much in interpretation (understanding) as it is in application (moral response). Mark Twain understood this well when he said, "Most people are bothered by those passages in Scripture which they cannot understand. The Scripture which troubles me most is the Scripture I do understand."

The Problem of Science and the Bible

The most frequently raised scientific issue, of course, is the question of evolution. We examined this briefly in the appendix to chapter 3; therefore little will be added here. Regardless of what position you hold, it is usually best to state that the Bible concentrates more on the *who* than on the *how* of creation. Scientists who acknowledge the authority of Scripture do not have a uniform view of the age of the earth, and they interpret the fossil evidence and the geological strata in different ways.

On the other hand, the speculations of some nontheistic evolutionists sometimes stretch beyond the limits of the scientific method as they conceive scenarios that are clearly contrary to the biblical world view. Forgetting the tentative nature of science, they make confident assertions about the genesis of life and man. But even if a theory demonstrates how something might have happened, this is a far cry from proving that it really did happen this way.

We must also remember that the Bible is not a scientific textbook, but when it does touch on scientific matters, it has proven to be trustworthy. In the past, two problems have contributed to misunderstanding about the scientific validity of the Bible. The first is the erroneous scientific conclusions drawn from the Bible by the church. The most notable error is the teaching that the sun and planets revolve around the earth. Some writers delight in referring to the trial of Galileo for his "heretical" notion that the sun may be the center of the solar system, but the Bible cannot be blamed for this blunder. The second cause of misunderstanding is that the Bible uses phenomenological language. That is, it describes nature as it appears to the eye. Thus, it speaks of sunrises and sunsets ("Its rising is from one end of the heavens, and its circuit to the other end of them; and there is nothing hidden from its heat" Ps. 19:6). But this does not teach that the sun rotates about the earth any more than today's scientist means this when *he* uses the term "sunrise" and "sunset."

Others say that the Bible is in error because it says that pi is equal to 3 instead of 3.14. They base this on 1 Kings 7:23 where a laver 10 cubits in diameter is given a circumference of 30 cubits. Comparing 7:23 with 7:26, however, it appears that the circumference was measured by using the inside diameter. The biblical phrase "the four corners of the earth" has been misunderstood to mean that the earth is flat with four literal corners. But Scripture uses this phrase figuratively, referring to all directions (Isa. 11:12; Ezek. 7:2; Rev. 7:1; 20:8).

When the Bible makes positive statements about the workings of nature, it is quite accurate, often running contrary to the erroneous concepts that were held in the time it was written. Job 36:27-29 gives an excellent description of the hydrologic cycle of evaporation, condensation, and precipitation. The statement about the earth in Job 26:7 was also far ahead of its time: "He stretches out the north over empty space, and hangs the earth on nothing." Other biblical statements about astronomy, biology, and medicine (e.g., the quarantine and sanitary laws of Leviticus) are equally remarkable.

Ethical Problems in the Bible
The three major ethical difficulties people have with the Bible are genocide, slavery, and the problem of evil, suffering, and hell. The third difficulty—hell—is the subject of the next chapter, so here we will confine our discussion to the problems of genocide and slavery.

The Bible presents the greatest set of ethical standards the world has ever known, focusing on love for God and one's neighbor. This makes God's genocidal command to utterly destroy the inhabitants of Canaan in Deuteronomy 20:10-18 (cf. Josh. 6:21) especially perplexing. There is no simple solution to this problem, but it can be substantially reduced by looking at it from several biblical perspectives: (1) It is easy to become so earthbound in our view of life that we forget that the author and giver of life has every right to take it away. (2) The sixth commandment is best translated "You shall not murder." This did not prohibit the taking of human life in fulfillment of the divine command for social justice in Israel (capital punishment) or for national defense. (3) The command to annihilate another nation (the Canaanites) was completely unique in Israel's history. (4)

Israel at this time was a theocracy, and there is no parallel for this in world history. (5) As a redeemed nation, the Children of Israel were to be distinct from all other nations. The idolatry and immorality of the Canaanites would have defiled them if Israel coexisted with them (Deut. 20:18). (6) God used the Israelites as His rod of judgment upon the Canaanites because of their gross immorality and wickedness. Archeological discoveries confirm that Canaan at this time was overrun with religious prostitution, infant sacrifice, bestiality, and many other abominations. Thus, the seeming cruel removal of the unrepentant Canaanites was not unlike the removal of a cancerous tumor.

Concerning the problem of slavery, here are three observations: (1) Slavery as we now understand it is quite different from the kind of slavery permitted in the Bible. Slaves were to be treated with human dignity and respect (Job 31:13-15), and if their masters violated their basic rights or abused them, they were to be set free (Ex. 21:26-27). If a slave ran away from his master, he was not to be mistreated or even returned (Deut. 23:15-16). Slaves were also allowed to participate in Israel's worship. (2) The institution of this system of slavery was a cultural phenomenon, designed to make the perpetuation of the patriarchal family unit economically feasible. This is foreign to our own culture, but it would be wrong to absolutize our own cultural values. (3) Although the New Testament also allowed for slavery, the epistles make it clear that all believers have an equal standing before the Father (Gal. 3:28). The reality of Christ was to transform every human relationship, and Christian principles cried out against the abuses of slavery.

Some people are troubled about the wrath of God and blood sacrifices. God is a God of love and mercy, but He is also a holy and righteous God. These divine attributes are found from Genesis to Revelation, and they are complementary, not contradictory. His love is a holy love, and His wrath is never capricious but always directed against sin and its dehumanizing results. The values of our society have become so diluted and distorted that the holiness of God and the sinfulness of sin have become foreign concepts to many. Concerning blood sacrifices, the New Testament makes it clear that they all pointed ahead to Christ, the Lamb of God sacrificed for the sins of the world. His crucifixion provided the greatest demonstration of both the love and the wrath of God that will ever be known.

The Problem of Apparent Errors

Almost all of the so-called contradictions in the Bible are due to differences in the perspective of the biblical writers when there is more than one account of a particular event. Close examination consistently reveals that the accounts supplement one another and that they can be harmonized. We see this in the alleged discrepancy in the Gospels concerning the number of angels at Jesus' tomb. Matthew and Mark report that one was there, but Luke and John speak of two. But if two angels were there, certainly one was there, and the one mentioned by Matthew and Mark was evidently more prominent. This is an example of selective reporting (all reporting is selective), and the same thing happens in other places (e.g., Mark and Luke mention only one demoniac who met Jesus near Gadara, but Matthew mentions two).

Another favorite example of a biblical contradiction relates to Genesis 1 and 2. Some claim these are two contradictory Creation accounts, but they can be harmonized when we notice two things: (1) Genesis 1 is a general survey of the six days of Creation, while Genesis 2 is a more detailed account of the sixth day of Creation, and (2) the name *Elohim* is used consistently in Genesis 1, because it emphasizes God's work as Creator, while the name *Yahweh* is used throughout Genesis 2 to underline the covenant relationship He establishes with man.

There are three basic causes for apparent errors in the Bible: sources, text, and interpretation.

(1) The biblical and extrabiblical *sources* are incomplete, and this can lead to the appearance of error. We mentioned how archeological discoveries confirm the biblical accounts about the Hittites and about Belshazzar. Similarly, Genesis was presumed to be in error when it mentioned the existence of the Philistines in the patriarchal period. But this was not an anachronism, because later discoveries revealed that the Philistines had an earlier history than was previously thought. The "error" was caused by incomplete sources, not biblical deficiency.

(2) Errors have crept into the biblical *text* through scribal mistakes and modernization. For example, 1 Kings 4:26 states that "Solomon had 40,000 stalls of horses for his chariots," but 2 Chronicles 9:25 says that the figure is 4,000. The exaggerated figure in 1 Kings is a common type of scribal error due to similarity in numerical notation

(also compare 2 Sam. 10:18 with 1 Chron. 19:18).

(3) Faulty *interpretation* of the biblical text and extrabiblical data can also cause the appearance of error. The *King James Version* of 2 Kings 23:29, for example, wrongly interpreted the Hebrew text to mean that Pharaoh Neco of Egypt "went up against" the king of Assyria. The text simply says "went up to," and this agrees with the Assyrian records which say that he went up to *aid* the Assyrians against the Babylonians. (Keep in mind that our English Bibles are *direct translations* from the original languages. A comparison of several translations often helps one gain a clearer understanding of the text.)

It would be wrong to say that all biblical discrepancies have been resolved, for a small number of problems still remain. But the increasing historical and archeological evidence has consistently been in favor of the Scriptures, and these problems should continue to diminish.

The Problem of Canonicity

How can you be sure that the people who decided which books should be included in the Bible were right? Couldn't the church councils have been mistaken? This objection reflects a misunderstanding about the nature of canonicity. The word *canon* means rule or standard, and it came to be used of the collection of books that conform to the standard of divine inspiration. Inspiration determines canonicity; the early church simply recognized these inspired books and rejected those books which did not bear the mark of inspiration. Thus, the church discovered the canonical books but did not determine them.

The canonical books of the *Old Testament* were divided into the Law, the Prophets, and the Writings (cf. Luke 24:44), and these had been recognized long before the time of Christ. Some books like Esther, Ecclesiastes, and Song of Solomon were disputed for certain reasons by a few rabbis, but the rabbinic council at Jamnia in A.D. 90 confirmed these long-recognized books. Some confusion was caused when, at some point, the Apocryphal books were added to the Septuagint, but these were not regarded as canonical by the Jews or the early Christian church. Jewish writers like Philo and Josephus never quoted from them, and neither did Jesus or any of the New Testament writers. It was not until the Council of Trent in 1546 (during the Counter-Reformation) that the Roman Catholic Church gave full canonical status to the Apocrypha.

The Apocryphal books were written more than 200 years after the time of Malachi, the last Old Testament prophet. Unlike the books of the Old Testament, they do not claim to have the prophetic stamp, and they do not manifest the authority and power of God. They are marred by doctrinal errors, subbiblical morality, and historical inaccuracies, and they were not originally received by the people of God.

The *New Testament* canonical books were progressively circulated and collected, and these 27 books were given official recognition by the councils of Hippo (A.D. 393) and Carthage (A.D. 397). All of these books passed the test of apostolic origin (e.g., Mark was an associate of Peter and Luke was an associate of Paul), apostolic date (first century), and apostolic doctrine.

The Problem of Miracles

This relates to the problem of science and the Bible because many object to the miracles of the Bible on scientific grounds. See chapter 4 for a discussion of how to deal with this issue. The Scriptures do not give us details about how God caused the 10 plagues to ravage Egypt, nor do they tell us how Jesus turned the water into wine or how He raised the dead. But it is clear that a supernatural agency was involved, and if God created the universe, He is certainly capable of accomplishing these things in the enactment of His redemptive purpose. Thus, God could easily appoint a sea creature and arrange to have it near the ship at the time Jonah was thrown into the Mediterranean Sea. There is no basis or need to allegorize the account of Jonah. Certain whales and sharks are capable of swallowing a man whole, and a few people have actually had such an experience and lived to tell about it. (James Bartley, for example, was removed alive from the gullet of a sperm whale in 1891 a day and a half after being swallowed. The whale had overturned Bartley's harpooning boat and his shipmates presumed he had drowned.) Whether God used an existing creature or created a new one for the purpose of delivering His Prophet Jonah is irrelevant, for God has the power to do both.

See Chart 25 for the second option to the question, "Is the Bible trustworthy?"

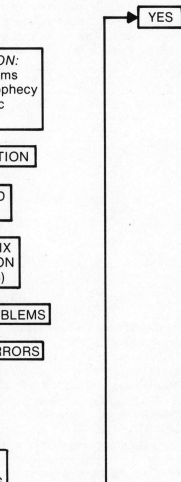

(CHART 25)

Third Option: The Bible Is Trustworthy

When a person acknowledges the authority of the Bible, he must have a clear picture of what the Bible says about the person and work of Christ. The Bible is not only authoritative, but its message is relevant to the earthly life and future destiny of all people. After we present the claims and credentials of Jesus Christ (see chapter 8), we should explain what it means to trust in Him (see chapter 13).

See Chart 26 for option three.

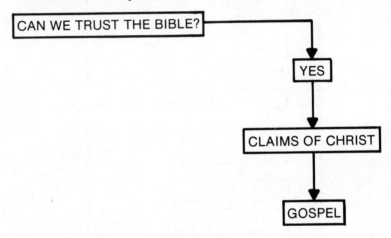

(CHART 26)

Summary and Flow Chart

The reliability of the Bible is a critical issue, because the Bible is the authority upon which the Christian world view is built. Some who reject the Scriptures do so because of false impressions about the transmission and content of the Bible. These misconceptions may need to be straightened out before a positive case for the reliability of the biblical documents can be made. This case is built upon the unique way in which the Old and New Testaments pass the bibliographic, internal, and external tests. It is sometimes appropriate to add a word about the uniqueness of the Bible and the great benefit it has brought to mankind.

If a person has no remaining objections to the Bible, you can present the claims and credentials of Jesus Christ, the Messiah

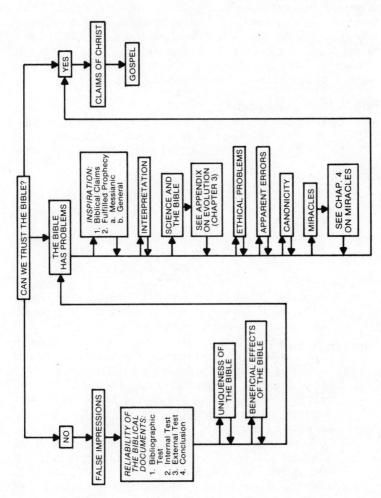

(CHART 27)

anticipated in the Old Testament and manifested in the New. But some people may still be troubled by certain problems that prevent them from acknowledging the authority of Scripture—e.g., problems of inspiration, interpretation, science and the Bible, biblical ethics, apparent errors, canonicity, and miracles. Handle these as succinctly as possible, but don't gloss over them. Naturally, it would be a rare person who is struggling with all seven of these areas, so it is only necessary to touch on the ones that appear to be causing the person difficulty in accepting the Bible as trustworthy.

Supplemental Reading

(1) F. F. Bruce, *The New Testament Documents: Are They Reliable?* (Eerdmans). An excellent application of the bibliographical, internal, and external tests to the New Testament documents.

(2) Norman L. Geisler, *Christian Apologetics* (Baker). Chapter 16 presents the historical reliability of the New Testament, and chapter 18 defends the inspiration and authority of the Bible.

(3) Norman L. Geisler and William E. Nix, *A General Introduction to the Bible* (Moody). Develops in detail the issues of biblical inspiration, canonization, and transmission.

(4) John McDowell, *Evidence That Demands a Verdict* (Here's Life). Good material on biblical reliability, prophecy, uniqueness, and canonicity.

(5) Josh McDowell and Don Stewart, *Answers to Tough Questions* (Here's Life). Offers brief answers to several specific questions about biblical reliability.

(6) John Warwick Montgomery, ed., *Christianity for the Tough Minded* (Bethany Fellowship). This book includes chapters on the issues of science and the Bible and the problem of genocide.

(7) John Warwick Montgomery, ed., *God's Inerrant Word* (Bethany Fellowship). A symposium of several scholars on the trustworthiness of Scripture.

(8) Bernard Ramm, *The Christian View of Science and Scripture* (Eerdmans). Contains many helpful insights on this complex issue.

(9) Bernard Ramm, *Protestant Christian Evidences* (Moody). A good discussion of fulfilled prophecy (chapter 3) and the supernatural character of the Bible (chapter 9).

(10) R. C. Sproul, *Objections answered* (Regal Books). Chapter 1 defends the reliability of Scripture.

(11) Clifford A. Wilson, *Rocks, Relics and Biblical Reliability* (Zondervan). A helpful and concise survey of the contribution of archeology to biblical studies.

7

Why Do the Innocent Suffer?

Often-Asked Questions:

If God is all-good and all-powerful, why did He make a world with so much suffering?

Why do innocent people suffer from things like disease and natural disaster?

If God is so good, loving, and powerful, why doesn't He put an end to suffering now?

How could a loving God send people to hell?

Did God create evil?

If God knew man would sin and bring evil into this world, why did He bother to create him in the first place?

Three Options

**WHY DO THE INNOCENT SUFFER?
OR, WHY DOES EVIL EXIST?**

| EVIL EXISTS; GOD DOESN'T | GOD EXISTS; EVIL DOESN'T | GOD EXISTS; EVIL EXISTS |

(CHART 28)

Traditionally we recognize two types of evil. The first is *moral evil*, caused by man through his rebellion against God and/or by his cruelty to others. The innocent suffer many times because of man's hatred (e.g., war), because of his overindulgence (e.g., the drunk driver who kills an innocent family), and because of his greed (e.g., many starving to death while others hoard surpluses).

The second is *natural evil,* a result of the natural phenomena inflicted on the innocent. Examples include hurricanes, plagues, earthquakes, and other diseases and disasters.

How do we account for the presence of both classes of evil, and is there an answer for the plight it presents?

The problem of evil is the old chestnut with which all philosophies and religions must wrestle. How to reconcile the concept of evil and God has baffled man for centuries. An examination of this problem reveals only three major alternatives: evil exists and God doesn't; God exists and evil doesn't; they both exist. Some people defend a perspective that allows for evil but not for God (atheism). Others seek to resolve the enigma by saying God exists but evil doesn't (pantheism). The third option states that both God and evil exist and there is an explanation for this predicament (theism). (See Chart 28.)

First Option: Evil Exists and God Doesn't

The atheist solves the problem by eliminating God. Evil and suffering are taken as givens, but the existence of God is not. Such prominent thinkers as David Hume, H. G. Wells, and Bertrand Russell have concluded, on the basis of their observations of suffering and evil, that the God of the Bible does not exist. Because of the prevalence of evil in the world, they formulated this classical proposition: (1) If God is all-good, He will destroy evil. (2) If God is all-powerful, He can destroy evil. (3) But evil is not destroyed. (4) Therefore, there is no all-good, all-powerful God.

This line of reasoning leads the atheist to deny God, but it can lead to two other conclusions. One conclusion says that God is all-powerful, but He is sadistic and, therefore, not all-good. There are no serious proponents of this view for, carried to its logical conclusion, it leads to atheism. Both the cruel-God view and the atheistic view reject the notion of a good God and hold to the reality of evil. The former attributes the evil to God whereas the atheist simply admits the existence of evil. The cruel-God position usually has been espoused by atheists writing satirically about theism.

The second conclusion says God exists and is all-good, but He is incapable of stopping evil and, therefore, He is not all-powerful. We will deal with this in the section on theistic views.

The false assumption made in this classical proposition is that evil would have to have been destroyed by now if God were capable or wanted to. On the contrary, if there is an all-good, all-powerful God, then the proposition could be stated another way: (1) If God is all-good, He will destroy evil. (2) If God is all-powerful, He can destroy evil. (3) Evil is not yet destroyed. (4) Therefore evil will be destroyed one day. See Revelation 20:10-15; 21:4; 22:3-8 for a description of how God plans to do just that.

Although we are specifically dealing with the problem of evil, it is critical that we re-examine atheism as a whole. To do this, see chapter 3 on the untenable nature of atheism and the evidence for the existence of God. When atheism is no longer seen as a viable option, we can move on to the second or third options.

See Chart 29 for the first option to this question.

Second Option: God Exists and Evil Doesn't

The pantheist argues that evil cannot be real if his view of God (God is all and all is God) is correct. The teachings of Vedanta Hinduism express evil as only a passing appearance, an illusion. There is only one reality, and that reality is good, regardless of how we perceive it. The illusion of evil is like thinking a coiled rope is a snake until one is close enough to see that it's only a rope. In America, the best known proponent of evil as an illusion is Christian Science.

There are two major objections to this alternative: (1) To accept it, we must deny our own senses and consistent personal experiences. All around us we see suffering resulting from evil. Man's inhumanity to man is apparent as we observe hatred, murders, robbery, famines, wars, etc. If we deny these, on what grounds can we verify the pantheist's position? If we can't trust our senses and experience in one area, how can we know that our senses and experience are not deceiving us when we accept pantheism?

(2) This viewpoint is contrary to two other kinds of evidence, scientific and historical. The evidence gathered through *scientific investigation* points to the reality of pain and suffering. Natural evil has been monitored for centuries and its existence has been universally verified. Scientists, with their investigative skills, have warned us accurately of impending disasters such as hurricanes, earthquakes, and tornadoes. Also, if pain were an illusion, the

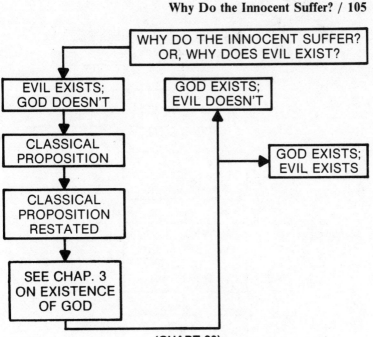

(CHART 29)

millions of dollars poured into research for disease control and cure would be worthless.

Legal historical evidence chronicles at every turn the reality of moral evil. Injustice, treachery, selfishness, and cruelty are boldly displayed on the pages of history. To deny evil would be to deny life as we know it. This is exactly what pantheists say they do, but in reality, their lives are no different from ours. They criticize falsehood and immorality just as we do.

The final and most important objection to this notion is that it contradicts the statements of Christ and the Bible (Jud. 2:11-15; Ps. 5:4-5; 51:2-5; Micah 3:1-3; Matt. 23:13-36; Gal. 5:19-26). For a closer look at the trustworthiness of Christ and the Bible, see chapters 4 and 6.

The second option is invalid because it violates our own personal experiences and reason, and it goes contrary to the testimony of Christ and the Bible, both of which we have shown to be true.

Chart 30 shows option two.

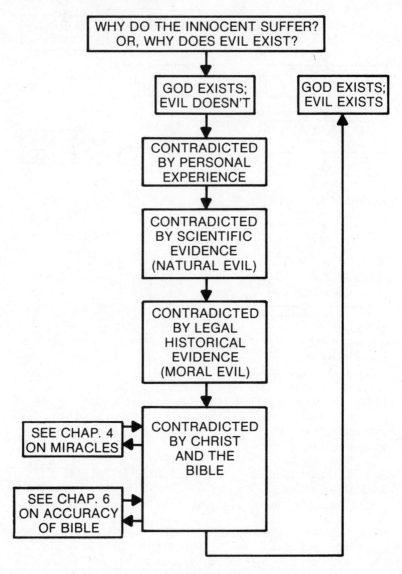

(CHART 30)

Third Option: God Exists and Evil Exists

We have three choices here. The first choice is finitism—evil is greater than God. The second choice is dualism—God and evil are co-eternal opposites. The third choice is theism—God is greater than evil and will one day defeat it.

Finitism. Philosophers such as Edgar S. Brightman and Peter Bertocci attempt to deal with the dilemma of God and evil by proposing a God who is finite in His powers and is thus unable to control or stop evil. God wants to aid us in our suffering, but He is not all-powerful and therefore helpless. When we look closely at this approach, we discover several pitfalls.

First, the finitist makes the same false assumption that the atheist makes. Both conjecture that God is incapable of defeating evil because He has not done it yet. Here is the finitist's line of reasoning: (1) God exists. (2) If God were all-powerful He would destroy evil. (3) Evil is not destroyed. (4) Therefore God is not all-powerful. Finitism fails to consider that God's timing is not human timing. The fact that God has not defeated evil today does not eliminate His ability to do it later.

Second, there could never be any hope of a solution. The finitist assumes that if man will join the conflict against evil and come to God's aid, ultimately man and God will win in the cause of good. But this assumption has no basis, for if a finite God cannot overcome evil, there is certainly no assurance that man's participation on the side of good will be the crowning blow that defeats evil.

Finally, and most importantly, this thesis is contrary to the Bible's position on both the character of God and how He intends to deal with evil. The Bible states in very clear terms that one of God's divine attributes is His omnipotence. Fifty-six times it declares that God is almighty (e.g., Rev. 19:6). The Bible also predicts that God will ultimately defeat evil (Rev. 21—22). For further documentation on the validity of the Bible, refer back to chapter 6.

The first choice under the third option is seen in Chart 31.

Dualism. Dualism assumes that God and evil are coeternal opposites. This view is similar to finitism because it rescues the goodness of God at the expense of His omnipotence. But dualism holds God to be equal with evil rather than less than evil. Although there are variations of this position from ancient Greek and Zoroastrian theology to modern-day process theology, all who hold

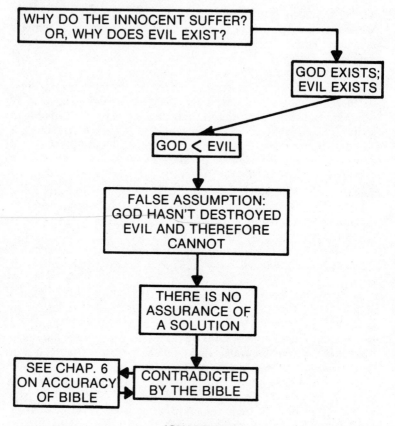

(CHART 31)

this view build it on the following premises:

The first premise for coeternality states that nothing can be the source of its opposite; light cannot be the source of darkness, or vice versa. The second premise states that evil is a thing, and if God were the only eternal source of all things, then He would be the cause of evil. Therefore, God and evil must exist together for all eternity or else God would be responsible for evil.

Both of these presuppositions are false. There are three problems with the first premise. First, it is possible for evil to occur out of good. This would not occur intrinsically but incidentally. A man may kill a dog while backing out of his driveway. There is nothing intrinsically evil about backing an automobile out of a driveway, but accidentally the animal is slain. Second, just because we have opposites, this does not mean that we have a first-cause opposite for each. For instance, take the concepts of fat and thin. They are opposites, but this doesn't necessitate an eternal fat as opposed to an eternal thin. Third, the concept of two ultimate forces that are in eternal opposition, each having the same amount of power, is not logical. Philosophers have presented this dilemma in terms of an absolute irresistible force coming in conflict with an absolute immovable object. If the force cannot move the object, it is no longer irresistible. If the object can be moved, it is no longer immovable. Either evil is greater than God, or God is greater than evil. It is logically absurd to have them as absolute coequals in eternal opposition.

We can prove the second premise false by demonstrating that evil is not a thing. Evil does not have an existence of its own; it is a corruption of that which already exists. We generally think of evil in negative terms—e.g., unsanitary, unhealthy, unreliable, uncivilized, incurable, etc. All these terms present evil as a negation of good.

St. Augustine and St. Thomas Aquinas both struggled with the identity of evil. They concluded that evil is real but not a substance in and of itself, because everything created by God is good. Evil, then, is an absence or privation of something good. Blindness was used as an example of the privation of sight. Aquinas noted that a thing is called evil for lacking a perfection it ought to have; to lack sight is evil in a man but not in a stone.

Evil does not exist by itself, because it does not exist apart from good. For example, rot can exist in a tree only as long as the tree exists. There is no such thing as a perfect state of rottenness. A rusting car and a decaying carcass illustrate the same point. Evil exists as a corruption of some good thing; it is a privation and does not have essence by itself.

The final and foremost reason for rejecting dualism is that it is contrary to the Bible. The Bible clearly affirms God's omnipotence and sovereignty, and its authors never recognize coeternal opposites in the universe. Moses describes the one sovereign God in Deuteronomy 4:35, and this is echoed by the Prophet Isaiah (Isa. 45:5). Christ Himself discussed the defeat of Satan in Luke 10:17-19. Scripture not only accounts for one sovereign almighty God, but also validates the statement that evil is a privation and not a thing in and of itself. Paul tells us in Colossians 1:16 that God created all things, and 1 Timothy 4:4 says that all things created were good.

The second choice under the third option is seen in Chart 32.

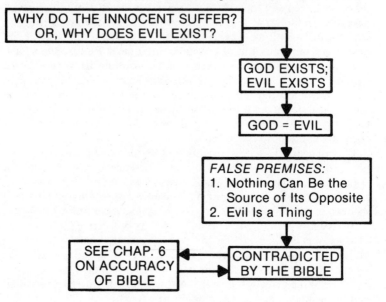

(CHART 32)

Theism. Theism stipulates that there is an all-good (Hab. 1:13), all-powerful (Rev. 4:8) God, who recognizes the reality of evil (Rom. 1:18-32), and will one day end evil and restore peace (Rev. 21:3-4). When the critic examines theism, he poses two difficult questions: (1) Why did an all-good, all-powerful God allow evil? (2) Why hasn't God put an end to evil?

The first question is one of *causation.* Why did God allow evil to occur in the first place? In answering this question, it is important to determine the point in time when evil entered history. This requires a summary of the biblical account of the origin of evil:

God created the universe without evil and suffering. He also created man perfect, with the ability to freely love or reject the God who created him (Gen. 1). Scripture says throughout that God desires to have loving fellowship with man (2 Chron. 16:9; Jer. 29:11; John 4:23; 1 Peter 3:18). But the ability to reject as well as accept is essential to any relationship. God did not force His love on man but gave him the privilege of a choice.

The magnitude of any choice is determined by the size of the consequences. Choosing between Coke and Pepsi is not a major choice in life, but choosing between apples and arsenic is. The consequences of accepting or rejecting God make this the choice of supreme importance. God told man that if he chose to embrace Him, their fellowship and blessings could continue. To spurn God and His commandments, however, would bring separation from Him (spiritual death) and physical death as well (Gen. 2). Genesis 3 tells us that man chose to go his own way rather than follow God's. Man thus suffered the consequences of spiritual and physical death. It was at this point that evil and suffering entered the world.

So we see that God did not create nor is He responsible for evil and sin. God's plan had the potential for evil when He gave man freedom of choice, but the actual origin of evil came as a result of man who directed his will away from God and toward his own selfish desires. Evil, remember, is not a thing but a corruption of a good thing already created by God. God told man what to do but man corrupted himself by choosing to disobey God. God's way is the perfect way and anything less than complete obedience to His instructions will bring problems into the process. God is not to blame for man's disobedience; man is the moral agent who is responsible.

Suppose, for example, a man purchases a $500,000 computer for his company. The manufacturer installs the computer and provides ample instructions as well as an operations manual. As soon as the computer personnel leaves, the new owner throws away the operations manual and ignores the instructions. He begins to randomly press buttons until the machine malfunctions and shuts down. The potential for misuse of the equipment was always there, but the manufacturer had given specific instructions on how to use it properly and had warned of the consequences of misuse. Whose fault is it that the machine broke down? God's creation had the potential for evil, but God did not promote it in any way. It only came about when man chose to ignore God's instructions and warning.

Because of the Fall, mankind became imperfect. This state of imperfection yielded temporal and eternal consequences.

The temporal consequences encompass both moral and natural evil. Moral evil is caused by man's inhumanity to man. Man in his fallen nature often seeks to promote himself at the expense of others. The suffering of innocent people is part of the insidiousness of evil. If only the wicked suffered, we would call that justice, but because there are innocent victims, there is a problem of injustice.

It is easy to associate moral evil with the fall of man, but how does the theist relate natural evil to the Fall? This occurs when the innocent are afflicted by natural phenomena such as typhoons and tornadoes. The Bible tells us that man's fall included not only a curse on him but also a curse on the creation around him (see Gen. 3:14-19; Rom. 8:18-23; Rev. 22:3). We live today in a disease-death environment. God did not originally design this environment; it has changed as a result of man's sin. This is an abnormal state which God will rectify when sin is removed (see Rev. 21:3-4; 22:3). Eden saw no natural disasters or death until after the sin of man, and there will be no natural disasters or death in the new heavens and earth when God puts an end to evil.

The temporal consequences are harsh, but the eternal consequences are even more grave, for they involve our relationship with God. Man was no longer a perfect being when he ceased to follow the perfect way of God (Rom. 3:23; Isa. 53:6; 59:2). The justice of God demanded that a penalty be paid for man's disobedience. The judgment for sin is eternal separation from the holy God (Rom. 6:23). This separation is defined by God as a confinement in hell forever (Matt. 25:46; Rev. 20:14-15). See the appendix for a discussion of three other issues that relate to this question (the fall of angels and men, the justice of hell, and the alternatives available to God when He created man).

Thus, human choice caused evil to enter our world and wrought temporal and eternal consequences upon mankind and his environment. Now we must turn to God's solution to man's problem of sin.

Two attributes of God's character must be kept in balance to understand how God resolves the dilemma. God's justice demands death as the penalty for the rejection of His command, and God's love seeks a solution to man's terminal condition. God cannot change the penalty because it is just, and it is in keeping with His character. But, out of His great love for His creation, He paid the penalty for man. God substituted Himself and made possible man's redemption from sin.

The story is told of a Tibetan ruler who once declared that anyone caught stealing would lose his hand to the ax. Throughout the kingdom, as violators were discovered, each was brought to the king and summarily lost his hand. One day guards brought an old woman before him, and when he asked her whether or not she had stolen the item, she responded affirmatively. He turned to her and said, "You have been found guilty as charged, and the penalty is the loss of a hand. I cannot change the verdict even though you are my mother, but my love for you is great, and I am willing to pay the price for you." And with that, he laid his hand on the chopping block and had it severed from his arm. His only choice was to substitute himself for one he loved. The woman was guilty and the penalty had to be paid. Had he excused her without payment he would have no longer been a just king.

Through substitution, God can satisfy both demands of His character. God is a righteous judge, and He cannot change His verdict on man's rebellion. What He did do, though, was offer to pay the penalty for us. Now the choice is up to us; we can pay the penalty ourselves, or accept the payment of our heavenly Father. The penalty *will* be paid. The only question is, "Who will pay it?"

God has still left us with the ability to accept or reject Him and His payment. But, as before, each choice has a consequence. If we accept God's payment and enter into a personal relationship with Christ, we are restored to fellowship and we are guaranteed eternal life. If we reject God's offer, we will spend eternity in separation from God.

Make sure you take the opportunity to make the Gospel clear at this point. For further help, refer to chapter 13.

We have established the cause of evil to be the disobedient choice of man. But there is still an unattended problem. Even if God didn't cause evil, why hasn't He stopped it? Before considering this, see Chart 33 for the causation part of the theism choice.

The first question was one of *causation,* and the second question is one of *cessation.* "Why hasn't God stopped evil if He can?" Most people want God to wipe out all evil that affects them, but they want to set the conditions for God's eradication process. They would like to see God eliminate the cruel world leaders, murderers, and thieves

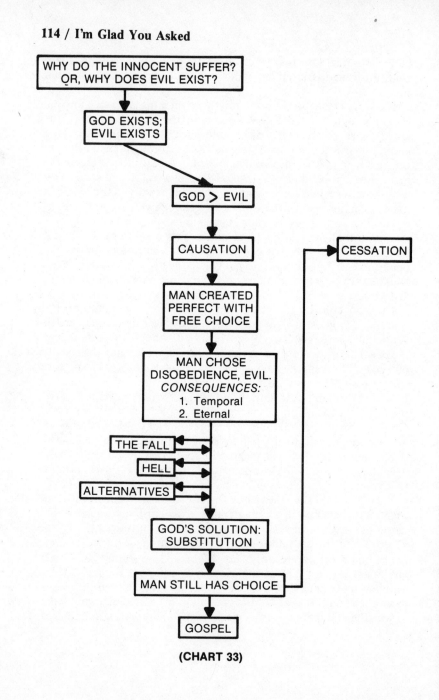

(CHART 33)

along with the natural disasters and diseases that afflict the world. But God is not interested in a partial containment of evil. He promised that He will someday permanently put an end to evil. To do this, He must not only move against actual evil but also potential evil.

Let's imagine that God stopped all evil at 12 o'clock. How many people would be left at 12:01? God showed us with Noah and the flood that if He removes actual evil and leaves potential evil behind, actual evil eventually returns. Even though God hasn't done it yet, we have God's promise that He will put an end to evil and suffering in the future (2 Peter 3:7-12; Rev. 19:1-2, 11-21; 20:7-15; 21:4-8).

(It can be helpful to consider what God would have to do in our present environment to eliminate the painful consequences of human choices. Every time an act of violence is attempted, God would have to make the weapons harmless. Bullets would turn to mush, clubs and knives would become soft, and so forth. If someone driving on a mountain road loses control on a turn, God would have to intervene, perhaps by lifting the car on a gust of wind and gently putting it back on the road. In effect, our lives would have to be cushioned by hundreds of miracles to protect us from the consequences of our actions.)

The Bible tells us that the world today is in an abnormal state. God did not begin creation with evil and suffering, and He will one day eliminate evil and suffering from His creation. God will return it to its normal state. So the question should not be, "Will God stop evil?" but, "When will He stop evil?"

Peter gives us a glimpse of why God is so patient. The early church suffered many persecutions and the Christians clung to the promise of Christ's return. They knew that suffering and pain would then end. Knowing this, they questioned Peter as to why it was taking Christ so long to come. Peter answered, "The Lord is not slow about His promise, as some count slowness, but is patient toward you, not wishing for any to perish but for all to come to repentance" (2 Peter 3:9). By delaying His return, Christ is extending the opportunity for people to turn to Him and thus escape eternal punishment. When Christ comes, there will be no more chances, for time will have run out. If a person has not accepted God's substitute before then, it will be too late.

It is imperative that we view temporal suffering in light of God's perspective. Believers are not in the land of the living going to the land of the dying. They are in the land of the dying going to the land of the living. One reason why God delays the return of Christ and allows temporal suffering to continue is to allow more people to hear about and accept Christ, and thereby escape eternal suffering. God could send Christ today and stop temporal suffering, but when He does, all opportunity to know Christ as Saviour goes with it. Pose this question to a friend who is concerned with why God allows suffering to continue: If God had sent Christ and eliminated all suffering the day before you had a chance to understand and accept Christ as Saviour, where would you be now? God delays putting an end to evil in order to allow us more opportunities to share the Gospel of Christ with others.

The following story illustrates how man refuses to see God's solution to evil:

A minister and a barber who boasted of being an atheist walked one day through a disreputable part of the city. As they looked around, the barber said, "This is why I can't believe in a God of love. If He is as kind as they say, why does He permit all this poverty, disease, and squalor? How can He allow all this drug-dealing and vandalism?"

The minister said nothing until they came across an unkempt and filthy man with hair down his back and a half inch of stubble on his face. Then he said to the atheist, "You can't be a very good barber or you wouldn't let people like this live around here without a haircut and a shave."

Indignantly, the barber answered, "Why blame me for that man's condition? I can't help it if he's like that. He's never given me a chance! If he would only come to my shop, I could fix him up and make him look like a gentleman!"

With a penetrating look, the minister said, "Then don't blame God for allowing these people to continue in their evil ways. He constantly invites them to come to Him and be changed. The reason they are slaves to sin and evil habits is because they refuse to accept the One who died to save and deliver them."

God is greater than evil, and He will indeed put an end to evil and suffering. Christ defeated evil through His work on the cross (1 Cor. 15:54-57) and will finalize that defeat by confining evil in hell forever.

The summary of the cessation part of the theism choice is shown in Chart 34.

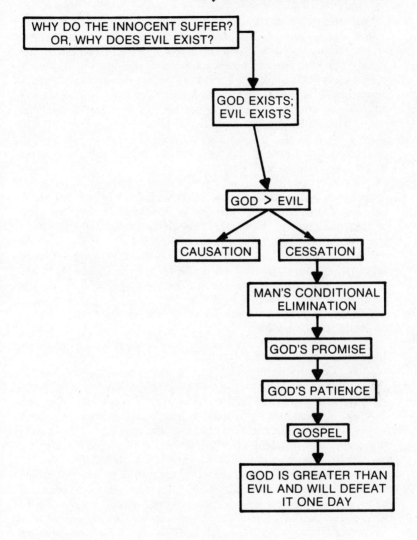

(CHART 34)

Was God the cause of evil? No! Man in his rebellion against God caused evil to enter this world. Why doesn't God stop evil now? He allows temporal evil to continue so that more may come to know Him. When God made His creation He knew that this world was not the best possible world, but it was *the best possible way to attain the best possible world.* At great personal sacrifice to Himself, God has counted and underwritten the cost of His creation. The story of the boy and his sailboat gives a clear picture of the sacrifice made by God for His creation:

The young boy used to play for hours by the lake with the sailboat he had carefully made. One day, a strong wind blew his boat away and he was heartbroken. Several weeks later when he passed a hobby shop, he noticed his sailboat in the window. He rushed inside and told the storekeeper that the sailboat in the window was his. The storekeeper replied, "That boat belongs to me now, and if you want it, you will have to buy it."

For six weeks the boy worked every job he could find and finally saved enough for the boat. Finally when he bought it, he walked out of the shop and said to his little boat, "I made you and I have bought you; you are now twice mine."

God is both our Creator and Redeemer, and He will forever receive the praise of His people.

Summary and Flow Chart

We have three possible solutions to the dilemma of the coexistence of God and evil. The first affirms the existence of evil but denies the existence of God. We restated the classical argument used to disprove God and showed how there could be an all-good, all-powerful God who will in the future put an end to evil. The major objection to this first option is that it denies God's existence. We referred to chapter 3 for a more detailed analysis of why atheism is untenable.

The second solution says that God exists but evil doesn't. If we think of evil as an illusion, we have to reject our own personal experience. The scientific evidence and the legal historical evidence verifies the reality of moral and natural evil. This position also requires a rejection of Christ and the Bible. Since the overwhelming evidence demonstrates the existence of evil, the second option is untenable.

The third possible solution allows for the existence of both God and evil. This leads to three more choices:

(1) *Evil is more powerful than God.* This rests on the assumption that God is unable to end evil because He has failed to do so thus far. This is a false assumption, and the position as a whole is contradictory to Scripture.

(2) *God and evil are coeternal and coequal.* Perceiving evil as a privation rather than a thing helps dispel this viewpoint. Not only is this choice erected on faulty logic but it also contradicts Scripture. The reliability of Scripture has been substantiated in chapter 6.

(3) *God is greater than evil.* We must ask two major questions here. First, "Why did God allow evil to begin with?" Second, "Why does God allow evil to continue?" Evil and suffering entered the world as a result of man's disobedience to God. God desired a loving relationship with man. Though created perfect, man could accept or reject God. He chose to reject God, and the consequences of this sin were both temporal and eternal. The temporal consequences included both moral and natural evil. The eternal consequences demanded that he be eternally separated from God. God's solution to man's problem was to substitute Himself for man on the cross, but each person must still make the choice of accepting or rejecting God's free offer of salvation.

Even though man's rebellion against God brought about evil, we still have to find out why God, who has the power, has not yet stopped evil. God allows temporal suffering to continue so that more can accept Christ and escape eternal suffering. The promise we have from God is that He will ultimately defeat evil and confine it even in hell. This third choice not only explains evil, but provides hope for the future.

Appendix on the Fall, Hell, and God's Alternatives

In the "Why do the innocent suffer?" question, there are three side issues that may need to be considered when exploring God's solution to man's problem. The three issues are: the fall of Satan, the justice of hell, and the alternatives available to God when He created man. We survey these topics in case they should ever come up in a discussion, but we should never raise more questions than a person asks.

The fall of angels and men. The original appearance of evil in the creation of God came through the choice of Satan. Satan and the other angels were spirit-beings whom God had created before the

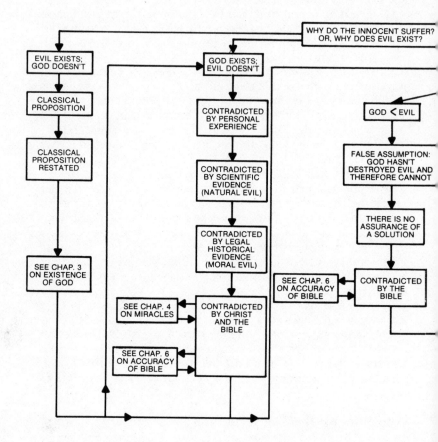

(CHART 35)

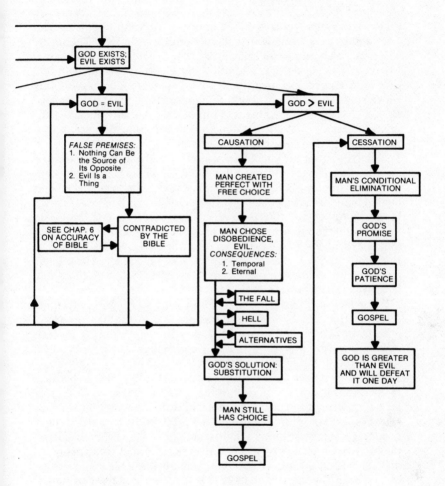

physical world of Genesis 1. They were created with the capacity of choosing whether or not to serve and love God. After a period of time, Satan and a group of other angels acted in willful disobedience. They chose to serve and love themselves rather than God. The angels who went with Satan are known today as fallen angels or demons. Many of the angels did not follow Satan but chose to continue following God; these angels still love and serve God today. Our conclusions about man's ability to choose also apply to the angels' choice. God allowed the potential for evil, but this did not make Him the producer of evil. The introduction of evil came as a result of a willful choice to disobey God.

Some time after the fall of Satan, God created man as a responsible moral agent. The tempter manifested himself in the Garden of Eden, and it was not long before the parents of the human race succumbed by pursuing their own course instead of God's. Man's fellowship with God was broken and thus evil and suffering entered our world. The major distinction between the fall of man and the fall of the angels is that all the angels ever in existence were alive when Satan disobeyed. But when man fell, there were only two humans in existence. Their imperfection was passed down as a result of their sin, and the whole human race was in need of salvation.

Someone once illustrated this problem by starting to button his shirt with the first button in the second hole. After that, all of the other buttons went into wrong holes as well. The story of Adam's fall became our story as well; sin is highly contagious. There is not only a social heredity but also a spiritual heredity of sin.

The justice of hell. Many people question the love of God because of the biblical concept of hell. Some would rather have God solve man's problem of separation by either allowing everyone into heaven (universalism) or by annihilating the wicked. Both alternatives stand in contrast to the testimony of Christ and the Bible. In His Sermon on the Mount, Christ described some attitudes that could send people to hell (Matt. 5:22). Later He explained that hell is a place of weeping and gnashing of teeth (Matt. 8:12; 25:30) as well as a place of eternal fire (Matt. 25:41) and punishment (Matt. 25:46). The Apostle Paul declared that the penalty for sin is eternal separation from God (Rom. 6:23). The concept of universalism is a violation of man's free choice. Hell is the consequence of man's rebellion against God. As we have said before, if you remove the consequences of a choice you no longer have a choice. If God brought everyone to heaven, He would do so against the wishes of many. C. S. Lewis once observed that there is a real sense in which the doors of hell are locked from the inside. While no one wants to be there, many will be there by their own choice. By rebelling against the will of God and rejecting His costly provision of salvation, they will continue forever in their rebellion and separation from God. If all people end up in heaven, there is no real consequence to sin and we don't really have free choice.

Which is the greater evidence of love: to let evil and suffering continue its ravages or to ultimately confine it? Evil must be contained, and hell is the place where God contains it. Suppose a group of terrorists walked into your home and killed your family. If they were apprehended by the police, would you consider it appropriate for the police to let them go or would you want the terrorists confined so they could kill no more? Obviously the more loving and just thing to do would be to contain the evil. Hell is required if justice and peace are to be restored in the kingdom of God.

To maintain a good garden, a gardener must periodically hoe out the weeds and carry them away. If he fails to preserve the garden in this way, it will soon be overrun by the weeds, and the garden will no longer exist. In the same way, if God does not remove the unrighteous, there will be no godly creation.

This separation from God is the just consequence of man's rebellion against God. Hell not only displays the justice of God, but it also displays His love. God's love is expressed best in His solution to the problem of hell, the giving of Himself as a substitute for man's penalty. But God did not force His love on man—He gave us a choice. No real exchange of love could take place between God and man without choice, for man would just be a robot. When the unbeliever chooses not to accept God's payment for his sin, God says, "My love for you recognizes your choice to be separated from Me, and thus I give you a place to exist in rebellion for all eternity." To the believer God says, "I love you so much that I will contain evil in hell forever so that peace and harmony can be restored to creation."

God does not send man to hell. Man sends himself by rejecting God's offer of salvation and restoration. Christ claimed He came not to send us but to save us from hell, if we would only believe (John 3:17).

Other options available to God. Since God knows everything, He knew that man would turn from Him. So why didn't He design His creation differently? Did God have any other options?

(1) *God could have chosen not to create man at all.* But God is worthy of all blessing, honor, glory, and dominion (Rev. 5:13), and it seems natural that His plan would allow for Him to display and receive glory. He is a loving God who desires to be loved back. In His omniscience, God knew that the best way to reveal His glory was to redeem a corrupt and wicked creation and make all things new.

(2) *God could have created man perfect and without choice.* But without responsible choice there is no capacity for love. Man would be a robot. Imagine getting up in the morning and finding yourself married to a robot. It could only respond in the way it was programmed. When you switch it on, it marches around saying, "I love you, I love you, I love you." No one would desire that kind of atmosphere for long. There would be no real communication, love, or response. The beauty of a loving relationship is that people love one another because of their own desire, and not because they are forced into it.

In analyzing God's options, we must remember that only God is omniscient, omnipotent, and all-good. Understanding this, we know that the option He chose was the best of all options for attaining His goals. But this does not mean that we are now in the best of all possible worlds. The best of all possible worlds is yet to come. There, man will have freedom, but a freedom not to sin. God says that the world in whch we live is the best possible way for us to obtain the best of all possible worlds. God's plan will bring the greatest good but not without costing God a great deal. Not only does He suffer as a result of His creatures' disobedience, but He also paid an unfathomable price, the cross, so that He could redeem sinful men.

Supplemental Reading

(1) Oliver R. Barclay, *Reasons for Faith* (InterVarsity Press). See chapter 4 for a good statement on the Christian perspective of evil.

(2) Kenneth Boa, *God, I Don't Understand* (Victor Books). Chapter 5 summarizes the dilemma of divine sovereignty and human responsibility and relates these to the problem of evil.

(3) Norman L. Geisler and Paul D. Feinberg, *Introduction to Philosophy* (Baker). Chapter 21 offers an excellent summary of the possible positions available when handling the problem of evil.

(4) Norman L. Geisler, *The Roots of Evil* (Zondervan). A very clear and concise presentation.

(5) Arlie J. Hoover, *The Case for Christian Theism* (Baker). A good overview of the problem can be found in chapter 17.

(6) Jon Tal Murphree, *A Loving God and a Suffering World* (InterVarsity Press). Gives new perspectives and practical helps.

(7) C. S. Lewis, *The Problem of Pain* (Macmillan). Lewis offers rich insights on this subject and this book is worth several readings.

(8) Gordon R. Lewis, *Judge For Yourself* (InterVarsity Press). See chapter 3 for a perspective on the problem of suffering.

(9) Bernard L. Ramm, *A Christian Appeal to Reason* (Word). See chapters 8 to 10.

(10) John W. Wenham, *The Goodness of God* (InterVarsity Press). An extensive treatment that draws principles from God's actions in the Old Testament. Wenham attacks the problem head-on and does not settle for simplistic answers.

8

Is Christ the Only Way to God?

Often-Asked Questions:

Isn't Christianity too narrow?

Since all religions are basically the same, does it matter what you believe?

Isn't the choice of which religion you take just a matter of personal preference?

An estimated 75 percent of the world are not Christians—can they all be wrong?

Christ can be the only way to God for you, but how can you claim that He is the only way for everybody?

Three Options

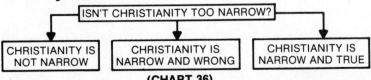

(CHART 36)

Tension mounts whenever there is a discussion regarding the exclusive claims of Christ. Since its beginning, orthodox Christianity has held that the only access to God is through Christ. At first glance this seems very arrogant and haughty. When we address the problem, we find three possible answers.

The first option denies that Christianity claims to be exclusive and narrow. Christianity is viewed as just one part of a grand mosaic that links God and man. The second option criticizes Christianity's claim to exclusivity, stating that it is wrong to hold such a position. If Christ is the only way to God, a lot of sincere people will be excluded. The third option is that Christianity is narrow but it is also correct (see Chart 36).

First Option: Christianity Is Not Narrow

The first option portrays Christianity as a very broad and accepting religion that would eliminate no one who sincerely seeks God. Christianity, according to some people, is just one of an assortment of religions. They believe that within this matrix of religions there are some technical distinctions, but all the religions are, in essence, the same. It doesn't matter how you get to God as long as you get there.

This concept has been portrayed in a number of ways. Some people see the journey to God as one of a series of caravans (different religions) seeking the same destination (God) from different directions. Others have represented God as the hub of a wheel with the spokes of the wheel representing the major world religions. Man can get to God regardless of which spoke he chooses. Still others see God sitting on top of a mountain, and the paths that lead to the peak are the different religions available to man. But such a broad and accepting view of Christianity does not account for the claims of Christ and His disciples, which are very exclusive.

According to the Bible, the concept that everyone is lost without Christ originates with Christ Himself. Consider these verses, for example, in which Christ eliminates alternative ways to God:

He who believes in Him is not judged; he who does not believe has been judged already, because he has not believed in the name of the only begotten Son of God (John 3:18).

I said therefore to you, that you shall die in your sins; for unless you believe that I am He, you shall die in your sins (John 8:24).

Jesus said to him, "I am the way, and the truth, and the life; no one comes to the Father, but through Me" (John 14:6).

Christ was unique among the founders of the world religions. Some promoted their teachings as the only way to God, but Christ promoted Himself as the only way to God. Christ claimed not only exclusivity but also deity. As the God-man, He boldly stated, "If you knew Me, you would know My Father also" (John 8:19). To know Him was to know God. Later Christ mentioned that all who had seen Him had seen God: "He who has seen Me has seen the Father" (John 14:9).

Another means Christ used to claim that He was God was the important phrase "I AM." For example, Jesus said, "Truly, truly, I say to you, before Abraham was born, I AM" (John 8:58). This was equivalent to claiming that He Himself was YHWH (Yahweh). Exodus 3:14 reads, "And God said to Moses, 'I AM WHO I AM'; and He said, 'Thus you shall say to the sons of Israel, "I AM has sent me to you."'" By calling Himself the I AM, Christ was at the same time claiming to be Jehovah God. (Three more I AM statements are found in 8:24, 28; 18:5.)

Christ supported His case for deity by ascribing to Himself various attributes of God. He claimed eternality (John 17:5) and omnipresence (Matt. 18:20 and 28:20). He also spoke of His sinlessness (John 8:46). His indirect claims included (1) *His acceptance of worship by men* (Matt. 14:33; John 9:35-39; 20:27-29); (2) *His ability to forgive sins* (Mark 2:5-11 and Luke 7:48-50); and (3) *His claim that all men would face Him in judgment* (John 5:24-28).

Christ clearly claimed to be the only way and His apostles affirmed this in their writings. Here are three examples:

> And there is salvation in no one else, for there is no other name under heaven that has been given among men, by which we must be saved (Acts 4:12).

> For the wages of sin is death, but the free gift of God is eternal life in Christ Jesus our Lord (Rom. 6:23).

> But even though we, or an angel from heaven, should preach to you a Gospel contrary to that which we have preached to you, let him be accursed (Gal. 1:8).

The apostles recognized that Christ was God as well as the only way to God. John made this clear by describing Him as "the Word"

(John 1:1, 14). Paul spoke of Christ as the one who created all things and who holds all things together through His divine power (Col. 1:16-17). He also addressed Jesus as "our great God and Saviour, Christ Jesus" (Titus 2:13).

Skeptics speculate that Christ could not have meant what the apostles understood Him to say. It is important that we understand that not only did His disciples hear Him proclaim His exclusivity and deity, but so did the critics of His day. Frequently when He made these dramatic claims, the Jews accused Him of blasphemy. They correctly understood the implications of what He was saying, realizing that He was making Himself to be an equal with God. This, of course, would indeed have been blasphemous if Christ's claims were not true (Mark 2:6-7; 14:61-64; John 5:18; 10:30-33). Many people today have tried to redefine the person and work of Christ in more general and broad terms. It is significant, however, that both His friends and His enemies recognized that He was claiming to be God and the sole means to God.

Christ taught that man was sinful and therefore separated from God. The only way for man to bridge the gap between himself and God was through his acceptance of Christ's payment for his sin. If we seek to bridge the gap through our own good deeds we will fall woefully short. All of the alternatives available to us apart from the sacrifice of Christ are based on systems of human effort and merit.

The death of Christ would have been a supreme blunder and a tragic waste if people could get into heaven by any other means ("for if righteousness comes through the Law, then Christ died needlessly," Gal. 2:21). Why would God make such a radical sacrifice if there was any other way? See chapter 11 for a detailed study on why our own good works are not sufficient to gain salvation.

If the Bible makes it so clear that Christ claimed to be God, and the only way to God, and His disciples affirmed his claims, how do people deny this? They do so because (1) they are ignorant of the Bible, or (2) they assume the Bible is in error. If their denial is due to ignorance, all we have to do is expose them to the teachings of Scripture. If it is due to a jaundiced view of the Bible, then we have to go back to the problem of the trustworthiness of the Bible (see chapter 6).

It is essential that we understand Christianity's position through the ages. Christ insisted that He was man's only solution for the problem of sin. That is a very narrow and restrictive assertion. The question no longer is whether or not Christianity is narrow, but whether it is right.

See Chart 37 for the first option.

Second Option: Christianity Is Narrow and Wrong

The second option recognizes that Christianity claims to be the only way to God but denies the validity of such a claim. The reasons for this rejection can be summarized in a series of assumptions. First, there are millions of sincere worshipers whose religions lay outside the confines given by Christianity. Second, truth is determined by one's beliefs or lack of belief, so even if Christ were right for us, it doesn't mean He is right for everyone. Third, Christianity is wrong because its exclusiveness makes it intolerant of other viewpoints. These assumptions must be dealt with if we hope to show that Christianity is both narrow and right.

The first major objection to Christianity's exclusiveness is that it eliminates many sincere people who are seeking God through other means. The assumption is that because these people are sincere, they can't be wrong. Sincerity, or the lack of it, however, has nothing to do with determining truth. We can be sincere and right or we can be sincere and wrong. We can cite numerous examples to show that sincerity by itself does not make something true. The people who followed Jim Jones to Guyana were sincere in their faith in Jones, but it was a misplaced faith. He led them to pain and death, not peace and prosperity.

A nurse in a large metropolitan hospital changed an oxygen tank in an oxygen tent for one of her patients. She went about her duties with the utmost sincerity, but on the next set of rounds another nurse found the patient dead. The tank she had affixed to the tent was filled with nitrogen, not oxygen. It had been improperly labeled at the warehouse. The nurse sincerely thought what she was attaching to the tent was oxygen, but it was not, and the consequences were deadly.

Some years ago, Jim Marshall of the Minnesota Vikings picked up a fumble and fought off tacklers repeatedly until he crossed the goal line. Marshall, however, crossed the wrong goal line and scored for the wrong team.

All these people were extremely sincere but they were sincerely wrong. Sincerity does not make something right or wrong. Truth

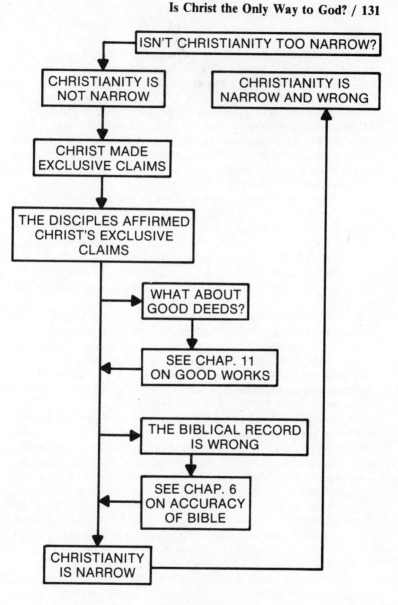

(CHART 37)

must be determined apart from sincerity.

A second major objection to Christianity is that, even though it can be right for us, it may not be right for everyone. This assumes that truth is determined by one's beliefs or lack of beliefs. People who raise this objection may tell you, for example, that some people enjoy raw oysters while others find them repulsive. Or they may say that the Ivy League look is sought after by some and rejected by others. The illustrations are always subjective decisions based on personal preferences and tastes. But the assumption that all truth is determined this way is false. Something is not objectively true just because someone does or doesn't believe in it.

For centuries, popular opinion stated that the earth was flat. Today, the scientific consensus is that the earth is spherical. Our understanding of the shape of the earth was arrived at by objective criteria, not by popular opinion. It is spherical, and our belief or lack of belief in that fact will not change it one bit. Similarly, the truth of Christianity cannot be determined on the basis of belief or lack of belief, but on the basis of objective criteria. For further study on this, see chapter 5.

A third objection is that Christianity is narrow and exclusive. The assumption here is that anything this narrow has to be wrong. Most of us were brought up to believe that toleration is a virtue. We learned catch phrases such as "different strokes for different folks," and "everyone needs to do his own thing." Since toleration is such an important concept today, we can understand why people think Christianity is too exclusive.

But the assumption behind this objection is not valid. A position can be narrow and wrong, or it can be narrow and right. Just being narrow doesn't make something either right or wrong. Someone once said, "Tolerance in personal relationships is a virtue, but tolerance in truth is a travesty." Truth is always intolerant of error. The fact that one plus one will always equal two is very narrow, but it is also right.

Life is full of examples of things that are narrow and true. For instance, when we fly in an airplane we want the pilot to land on the runway, not the highway; to land right side up and not upside down; and to land when he is told, not before or after.

Suppose someone feels that the automakers are cramping his style by specifying "unleaded fuel only" for his automobile. If he resisted this narrow confine by using diesel fuel or, worse yet, water, his car would fail to operate. The specifications may be narrow, but nevertheless they are valid.

We know about the claims of Christianity, but it would be helpful to compare them with those of the other major world religions. Whenever we hear someone say "all religions are basically the same," we immediately know that the person has little in-depth knowledge of the various religions. We also know that the person is probably not intimately involved in any one religion, otherwise he would at least know the distinctives of his own.

The major religions differ in their perception of who God is, in their view of ultimate human destiny, and in their means of attaining salvation. To see this, consider five great world religions: Hinduism, Buddhism, Judaism, Islam, and Christianity.

Let's look first at the different views of God. The Christian is a trinitarian. He believes in only one true God, but in the unity of the Godhead there are three eternal and coequal Persons. The Jew and the Muslim are strong unitarians. They believe in only one true God and only one Person in the Godhead. The philosophical Hindu is a monist (all is one) or pantheist whose god is an eternal, nonpersonal, abstract being without knowable attributes. God is an It rather than a Person. The popular sects of Hinduism are polytheistic, worshipers of many gods. Various sects of Buddhism hold a variety of views on God. These sects are either polytheistic, pantheistic, or atheistic. As we can see, there is a great divergence in views just on the identity of God.

Next, we can draw our attention to the issue of man's destiny. Where is man headed when life is finally over? For the Christian, believers will spend eternity in heaven. There, they will experience a personal existence and have fellowship with God forever. Among Jews today we find a broad spectrum of views on man's destiny. Many say that nothing exists after this life is over. Others believe they will go to life hereafter that will be enjoyed in the company of their Messiah. Muslims believe they will join Allah in heaven for an eternity of sensual pleasure and gratification. Hindus believe they eventually will end up becoming one with the impersonal supreme being (Brahman) in a state of nirvana. The individual ceases to have his own personal identity or existence. Buddhists aspire to nirvana as a state of total nothingness, a final annihilation of individual consciousness. On the surface, each of these religions speaks of an ultimate destiny for man, but that destiny is vastly different.

How does man achieve his destiny in each of the major religions? According to Christianity, he enters heaven by his acceptance of Christ's payment on the cross for his sin. Christianity's solution is based on faith in Jesus Christ, not on man's good works.

The Jew believes he gains salvation by turning back to God and living a moral life. There is no assurance of salvation since it will be determined by man's own efforts. The Muslim tries to earn his own salvation by believing in the five doctrines of Islam and by performing the duties of the Five Pillars of faith. But it all depends on his behavior, so he cannot be sure.

The Hindu believes he achieves his desired state of oneness with Brahman through a series of reincarnations. The law of karma says a Hindu reaps in the next life the rewards or punishments of the present life. The Buddhist believes he earns his own release from the endless chain of reincarnations by following the Four Noble Truths and the Eightfold Path.

Four of these five religions seek salvation through human effort, but the effort is different for each. Christianity recognizes the frustration and futility of man's own efforts and declares that man's salvation rests in the provision and grace of God.

The major religions differ in their perspectives of God, man's destiny, and the means of salvation, and they are all narrow as well. They all claim to be right. Christianity is not the only religion with exclusive claims. Jews, Muslims, and Buddhists all believe they have found the only true way to God. Hindus are the only ones who might equivocate on an exclusivity clause. Ramakrishna stated that "many faiths are but different paths leading to one reality, God." On the surface, it appears that Hindus allow for different ways to get to nirvana.

A closer look at Hinduism reveals that the Hindu allows for an openness to other faiths but stresses the superiority of his own. If all faiths are but different paths, we might wonder if the Hindu would allow his children to be brought up as Christians. There is really only one path by which an outsider can enter the fold. He must live a pious life and then, after many transmigrations, his soul may be at last reborn into a Hindu family.

The Hindu also assumes that all religions are different paths on a mountain, heading upward in the same direction, all worshiping the same God. If we have learned anything in our quick survey of these five major religions, we have learned that they aren't even on the same mountain.

Each of these religions seeks to answer man's questions regarding his origin, destiny, and current role in the universe. Their answers, though similar at first glance, are dramatically different when scrutinized closely. How can all of these religions be right at the same time? They disagree with each other in the three major issues of who God is, where man is going, and how he is going to get there. How can we square Hinduism's teaching that God is impersonal with Christianity's teaching that God is personal? How can there be three Persons in the Godhead and yet only one Person in the Godhead? These questions are only the tip of the iceberg of contradictions among the major religions.

The law of noncontradiction will help us at this point. This most basic law of logic, simply stated, says that if two statements about one particular issue contradict each other, then (1) only one of them is true, or (2) they are both false. They cannot both be true in the same sense and at the same time. If statement A contradicts statement B:

Either A is true and B is false,
or A is false and B is true,
or A is false and B is false.

If someone says, "All dogs shed hair," and another person says, "Poodles don't shed hair," then either both are wrong or one is right. They both can't be right. If Christ claims to be the only way to God and Mohammed says there is another way to God, then either Christ is right and Mohammed is wrong, or Christ is wrong and Mohammed is right, or they are both wrong. They cannot both be right.

Since the major religions contradict one another, we can apply the law of noncontradiction. Either one of them is right and the rest are wrong, or they all are wrong; they cannot all be right.

We stated earlier that the hard question facing Christianity was not whether it is narrow, but whether it is true. The exclusiveness of Christ's claims is no reason to declare Him wrong. We must proceed to our third option where we will analyze whether or not Christianity is true.

The second option is depicted in Chart 38.

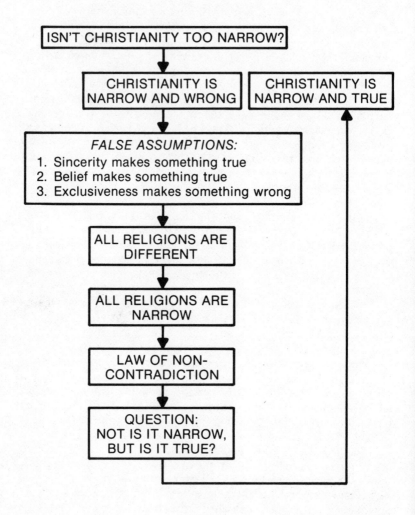

(CHART 38)

Third Option: Christianity Is Narrow and True

We know from Christ's own claims that Christianity is narrow. What we must determine now is whether or not Christianity is true. If Christ was not who He claimed to be, then we are left with some very uncomfortable alternatives. If Christ was not the only way to God, He was either a liar or a lunatic. Neither of these choices is very palatable, but they are our only options if Christ was not Lord of all. Christ was not merely a good man or a great teacher.

The very character of Christ argues persuasively against His being a liar. He spoke of truth and virtue on every occasion. His life exemplified the very message He proclaimed. In fact, very few people will make this claim. The evidence is weighted heavily in favor of Christ being a paragon of truth and virtue rather than a liar.

The consistent life and testimony of Christ make it clear as well that He was not a lunatic. A lunatic displays abnormalities and imbalance as a part of his lifestyle. When we analyze the life of Christ we do not find inconsistencies and imbalance. To the contrary, we discover a man who is mentally sound and balanced.

If Christ is not a liar nor a lunatic, then He is who He claimed to be—Lord of all, the only way by which man can be saved. The objective data for the truth of Christianity comes from two sources— the Bible and the legal historical evidence for the Resurrection—and we have already supported the truth of both these sources. See chapter 6 for information regarding the reliability of the Bible, and see the appendix of chapter 4 for a detailed explanation of the evidence for the Resurrection.

Incidentally, it is often helpful to use a diagram to present the claims and credentials of Christ. In Chart 39 the left column lists some of the unique claims He made, and the right lists some of His credentials that back up His claims.

His works (credentials) authenticate His words (claims), and the nature of His claims leads us to the liar, lunatic, Lord trilemma, because these are the only real options about Jesus. (A fourth option that He was a legend was refuted in the appendix to chapter 4 and in chapter 6.)

Even though there is ample evidence in favor of the truth of Christianity, there are still a couple of questions that may need to be addressed. The first concerns the Jew. Many people assume that Christianity is a Gentile religion or that to become a Christian, a Jew

UNIQUE CLAIMS OF CHRIST	CREDENTIALS OF CHRIST
—Claimed to have power to forgive sins. —Claimed to be sinless. —Claimed to fulfill Old Testament messianic prophecies. —Claimed that He would rise from the dead and raise all men. —Claimed that He would come again and judge the world. —Claimed to be the exclusive way to salvation.	—His sinless life (even His enemies had to acknowledge this). —His miracles (power over nature, disease, demons, death). —His unique character and teaching. —His fulfillment of hundreds of messianic prophecies. —His power to change lives. —His resurrection from the dead.

(CHART 39)

must stop being a Jew. Others have raised this issue because Jews worship the one true God of Abraham. So why aren't they going to heaven?

In the early church, the problem facing believers was not how a Jew could become a Christian but how a Gentile could become a Christian. Early Christianity was predominantly Jewish. The only people who were Christians in Acts 2 were Jews. When a Gentile named Cornelius became a Christian in Acts 10, the Jewish Christians had difficulty believing it was possible. Jesus was a Jew, as were all of the apostles. Paul tells us in Philippians 3:4-11 how he needed Christ for salvation even though he was the epitome of a good Jew. Every one of the New Testament writers, with the exception of Luke, were Jews. The New Testament revealed that in Christ, Jews and Gentiles could come together into one body without distinction.

> For I am not ashamed of the Gospel, for it is the power of God for salvation to everyone who believes, to the Jew first and also to the Greek (Rom. 1:16).

> There is neither Jew nor Greek, there is neither slave nor free man, there is neither male nor female; for you are all one in Christ Jesus (Gal. 3:28).

> For He Himself is our peace, who made both groups into one, and broke down the barrier of the dividing wall (Eph. 2:14).

For there is one God, and one Mediator also between
God and men, the man Christ Jesus (1 Tim. 2:5).

It is important for Jewish people to know that to become
Christians, they do not have to forsake their Jewishness any more
than Irishmen would have to forsake being Irish. There are Gentile
Christians and Hebrew Christians. A Jew does not have to abandon
his heritage to become a Christian.

The Jew, just like any other man, must deal with his sin and the
separation it has caused between him and God. The standard set by
God is perfection, and the Jew doesn't measure up to that standard
any better than the Gentile does (Isa. 53:6). Paul, "a Hebrew of
Hebrews," speaks of the common dilemma in Romans 3:9-10: "What
then? Are we better than they? Not at all; for we have already charged
that both Jews and Greeks are all under sin; as it is written, 'There is
none righteous, not even one.'" The penalty for this imperfection is
death and separation from God.

What is the solution to man's problem of sin? Man can pay the
penalty himself or accept a substitute in his place. (The futility of
seeking to pay the debt with our own efforts is examined in chapter
11.) In the Old Testament, man escaped the penalty of his sin by
presenting an unblemished animal as a sacrifice in his stead. But the
debt was only covered, not canceled, and the next year on the Day of
Atonement it had to be covered again. Christ said His sacrifice of
Himself ended for all time the need for another sacrifice. He canceled
the debt for all who would come to Him.

Imagine that you have just borrowed $1,000,000 and the bank
discovers you cannot pay it back. Perhaps you can pay the interest,
but you have no means of reducing the principal. Then someone
comes along and not only pays the current interest payment but pays
the principal as well. At that point, your debt is canceled and you are
again financially solvent. Christ paid not only the interest but also the
principal on our debt of sin. All we have to do is accept that payment.

This is all the Jew must do as well. He must come to a personal
relationship with Jesus if he wants to be reconciled to God. Romans
3:29-30 says, "Or is God the God of Jews only? Is He not the God of
Gentiles also? Yes, of Gentiles also, since indeed God who will justify
the circumcised by faith and the uncircumcised through faith is one."
The God of all creation makes salvation available for all people
through His Son Jesus.

Many believe that Christianity's exclusion of Judaism as a way to God is just nit-picking. Their problem can be stated in this way:

(1) Judaism worships the one true God in the Old Testament.

(2) Christianity proclaims Christ and the God of the Old Testament as one.

(3) Therefore, Judaism in reality believes in the same God.

But what is not understood here is that the Jew rejects Christ as the Son of God, so the proposition should be stated in this way:

(1) Judaism rejects Christ as the Son of God.

(2) Christ is the Son of God and the only way to the Father.

(3) Therefore, Judaism in reality has rejected the only way to the Father.

Either Christ is right or wrong. If He is right, and we have tried to show that He is, then the Jew must come through Him to get to God.

A second question we sometimes hear concerns the proclamation of Christianity to others. Because of the great missionary mindset of Christianity, the question is posed, "Isn't it unloving, intolerant, condescending, even arrogant, to preach that Christ is the only way to God?"

To some people Christianity appears harsh and unloving. We must balance this negative reaction with two crucial points:

(1) It was the same Christ who said He was the only way (John 14:6), and who gave the Great Commission to take this message to everyone (Matt. 28:19-20; Mark 16:15; Luke 24:47; Acts 1:8).

(2) Since Christianity is true, even though it is narrow, it would be unloving if we didn't share Christ's solution with others.

We can illustrate this by imagining a scientist who has just discovered a complete cure for cancer. He now faces the dilemma of whether he should share his discovery. If he shares it, he risks offending some who are seeking other techniques to cure the problem. The scientist will challenge the theories of other researchers when he shares his discovery and thus risk their scorn. But since his only alternative is to let people die in their ignorance, the loving thing would be to share the cure, even though some might misunderstand the offer. Likewise, the world has need of Christ and we must lovingly share Him with people.

In all this, we must remember to expose Christianity to others—not impose it. Christ never called us to force Him on anyone. Our task is to present Christ in a loving way and allow men and women the

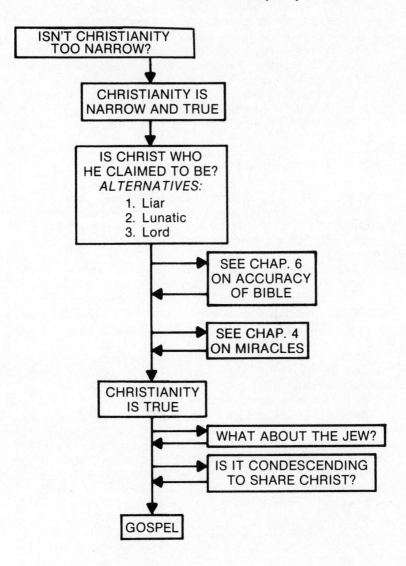

(CHART 40)

choice of accepting or rejecting Him.

If these two supplementary questions are not raised by your non-Christian friend, you can move right into a presentation of the Gospel. It is not enough for a person to recognize intellectually that Christ is the only payment available for sins. He must personally accept Christ as his own Saviour from sin. For a detailed presentation of what is essential for salvation, refer to chapter 13.

The section on Christianity as narrow and true is shown in Chart 40.

Summary and Flow Chart

The first option we considered is that Christianity is not narrow, but then we faced the problem that Christ claimed not only to be the exclusive way to God but also to be God Himself. The disciples also affirmed what Christ taught. When the question arose, "Where do good deeds fit in if salvation comes through Christ alone?" we referred to chapter 11.

If, after being exposed to Christ's claims in Scripture, a person persists in denying the truth of such testimony, then his problem is not with this question but with the question addressed in chapter 6, "Is the Bible reliable?" The testimony is clear that Christ claimed to be the only way. A person must decide if he believes this claim is true or false.

The second option we looked at is that Christianity is narrow and wrong. We found the assumptions behind this option to be false. Truth is not determined on the basis of sincerity or beliefs. Nor can a faith be discredited simply because it is narrow.

After a brief examination of five major religions, we concluded that, contrary to popular belief, they are all different and not basically the same. We also noted that Christianity is not the only religion that claims to be the only right one. Then with help of the law of noncontradiction, we saw that either one and only one of the religions of the world is right, or they are all wrong; no two of them can be right. This left us with the task of determining if Christianity is true.

The third option claimed that Christianity is both narrow and true. The unique claims of Christ lead to only three alternatives: He was a liar, a lunatic, or the Lord. The evidence from the Bible and the Resurrection give sufficient objective data to warrant a positive

ISN'T CHRISTIANITY TOO NARROW?

CHRISTIANITY IS NARROW AND TRUE

IS CHRIST WHO HE CLAIMED TO BE? *ALTERNATIVES:*
1. Liar
2. Lunatic
3. Lord

SEE CHAP. 6 ON ACCURACY OF BIBLE

SEE CHAP. 4 ON MIRACLES

CHRISTIANITY IS TRUE

WHAT ABOUT THE JEW?

IS IT CONDESCENDING TO SHARE CHRIST?

GOSPEL

CHRISTIANITY IS NARROW AND WRONG

FALSE ASSUMPTIONS:
1. Sincerity makes something true
2. Belief makes something true
3. Exclusiveness makes something wrong

ALL RELIGIONS ARE DIFFERENT

ALL RELIGIONS ARE NARROW

LAW OF NON-CONTRADICTION

QUESTION: NOT IS IT NARROW, BUT IS IT TRUE?

CHRISTIANITY IS NOT NARROW

CHRIST MADE EXCLUSIVE CLAIMS

THE DISCIPLES AFFIRMED CHRIST'S EXCLUSIVE CLAIMS

WHAT ABOUT GOOD DEEDS?

SEE CHAP. 11 ON GOOD WORKS

THE BIBLICAL RECORD IS WRONG

SEE CHAP. 6 ON ACCURACY OF BIBLE

CHRISTIANITY IS NARROW

(CHART 41)

response to the question of the truthfulness of Christ.

Two other questions might have to be worked through before the Gospel is presented: "What about the Jews—do they need Christ?" and "Is it condescending to share Christ with others in the world?"

We concluded finally that Christianity is narrow and right because it is true. Without Christ there is no solution to man's problem of sin and separation from God.

Supplemental Reading

(1) J. N. D. Anderson, *Christianity and Comparative Religion* (Tyndale). An insightful presentation of the uniqueness of Christianity.

(2) Kenneth Boa, *Cults, World Religions, and You* (Victor Books). Examines 10 major world religions, giving background, teachings, and biblical evaluation.

(3) David A. DeWitt, *Answering the Tough Ones* (Moody). Chapter 1 shares a true experience of how this question was handled with a non-Christian.

(4) Gordon R. Lewis, *Judge For Yourself* (InterVarsity Press). Chapter 1 is helpful in showing how appropriate Scripture passages apply to different aspects of this question.

(5) R. C. Sproul, *Objections Answered* (Regal Books). Chapter 2 briefly traces the idea of toleration in our culture as a clue to the concept of the equal validity of all religions.

(6) Barry Wood, *Questions Non-Christians Ask* (Revell). Chapter 6 on Jesus and the Jew and chapter 8 on Jesus and Mohammed give some hints on witnessing to both groups.

9

Will God Judge Those Who Never Heard About Christ?

Often-Asked Questions:

Would God condemn an innocent heathen simply because he never heard about Christ?

What about religious people who don't know about Christ and call their god by a different name?

What happened to people before the coming of Christ?

What about infants and people who are mentally incapable of understanding the Gospel?

Three Options

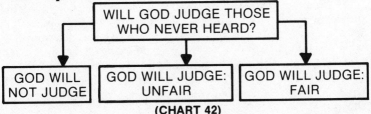

(CHART 42)

Some try to minimize this problem by arguing that those who have not heard about Christ are innocent because of their ignorance and will not be judged. If, on the other hand, these people are subject to divine judgment, there are only two remaining possibilities—God's judgment is either unfair or fair. Many question the justice of God at this point because they falsely assume that God will hold people accountable for that which they have no way of knowing. But the Scriptures are clear that God's judgment is perfectly just and that no one who stands before God will accuse Him of being unfair.

First Option: God Will Not Judge Those Who Have Not Heard

The objection in this chapter is closely related to the conclusion of the preceding chapter, that Christ is indeed the only way to the Father (John 14:6; Acts 4:12). When a person begins to grasp the exclusiveness of the Gospel, it is only logical that one of the variant questions listed at the beginning of this chapter would surface in his mind. In some cases this objection may be raised as an evasive maneuver when the implications of the Gospel are beginning to get too close to home. More often, however, it comes up because it makes God appear to be an unjust judge. Something would be desperately wrong if humans showed more compassion than God for those who are lost.

These concerns have led some people to the conclusion that those who have never heard about Christ will escape the judgment of God. If this is true, Christian missionaries are not only wasting their lives but may be doing great harm. By preaching the Gospel to those who were unaware of Christ, they have brought people from a state of innocence to a state of moral culpability if they do not respond. This would mean that passages such as the Great Commission (Matt. 28:19-20) and Romans 10:14-15 make no sense at all. The death and resurrection of Jesus Christ should have been kept a secret!

As we saw in chapter 7, the Bible is clear on the reality of divine judgment and hell. The position of universalism (all people will be saved) is naturally more appealing, but reality is not determined by what we would like to be true. It is determined by the infinite mind of God who said, "For My thoughts are not your thoughts, neither are your ways My ways . . . For as the heavens are higher than the earth, so are My ways higher than your ways, and My thoughts than your thoughts" (Isa. 55:8-9).

The supreme authority for truth is divine revelation, not human opinion. God did not choose to disclose many details we would like to know, but the Scriptures offer enough principles to enable us to gain a reasonably accurate perspective on this question. (We assume here that the objector has already come to acknowledge the trustworthiness of Scripture. If not, he may question some of these biblical principles. When this happens, you may have to review some of the material in chapter 6 before going on.)

The following paragraph summarizes the scriptural teaching on the love and holiness of God. Judgment is necessary because of His character.

God is love (1 John 4:8), and this love was manifested when He "sent His Son to be the propitiation [satisfaction] for our sins" (1 John 4:10). "We know love by this, that He laid down His life for us" (1 John 3:16; also see Rom. 5:5-8). God wants no one to spend an eternity apart from Him but "desires all men to be saved and to come to the knowledge of the truth" (1 Tim. 2:4). The Lord is "compassionate and gracious, slow to anger, and abounding in lovingkindness and truth" (Ex. 34:6); it is not His desire that any should perish, but that all should come to repentance (2 Peter 3:9; cf. Deut. 30:19; Ezek. 18:23, 32). God is not only loving and merciful, but He is also holy and just, and, therefore, He cannot overlook sin. Sin is a universal human condition (1 Kings 8:46; Ps. 51:5; Rom. 3:9, 23; 1 John 1:8), and it causes a breach between man and God (Isa. 59:2). Sin leads to death (Rom. 6:23), and the wrath of God abides on all who are separate from Christ (John 3:18, 36). All have sinned, and those who have not been "justified as a gift by His grace through the redemption which is in Christ Jesus" (Rom. 3:24) are under divine condemnation (Rom. 3:10-20; 5:16-19) and must stand before God in judgment (John 5:27-29; Rev. 20:11-15). Human works, sincerity, and religion are not enough to avert this judgment, because apart from Christ we are enemies of God (Rom. 5:10). Only through Christ can a person be saved from the wrath of God (Rom. 5:1; 8:1).

People are not lost because they have not heard. They are lost because they are sinners. We die because of disease, not because of ignorance of the proper cure.

When the first option is overcome, it automatically leads to the second shown in Chart 43.

Second Option: God's Judgment of Those Who Have Not Heard Is Unfair

When a person realizes that God *will* judge the heathen, he might object that this is unfair. He might also raise questions about the justice of God and the ignorance of man. We will look at both of these.

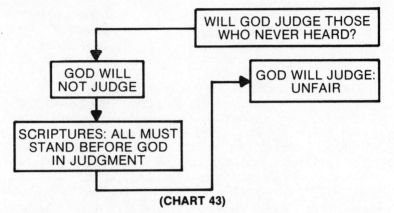

(CHART 43)

The perfect justice of God. If God is loving and fair, can He really condemn people who haven't had a chance to make a decision about Jesus Christ? If He does judge them, how can we commit ourselves to such a God?

While the Bible does not develop the theme of those who have not heard as deeply as we would like, it does provide several principles we can use in responding to this important objection. One of these is that God is holy and just in all His ways: "Surely, God will not act wickedly, and the Almighty will not pervert justice" (Job 34:12). God has "fixed a day in which He will judge the world in righteousness" (Acts 17:31; also see Gen. 18:25—"Shall not the Judge of all the earth deal justly?"—and Rom. 3:3-5). On that day, no one will defiantly accuse God of injustice.

Romans 2:2-16 reveals three important aspects of the judgment of God: (1) God judges according to truth (Rom. 2:2-5). Unlike a human judge, God knows the complete truth (including the thoughts and intentions of the heart; Heb. 4:12), and His justice is not clouded by error. (2) God judges according to works (Rom. 2:6-10). His judgment is contingent on whether a person obeys the truth or obeys unrighteousness. (3) God judges according to impartiality (Rom. 2:11-16). "There is no partiality with God" (Rom. 2:11; see 1 Peter 1:17).

Another key principle in answering this question is that God's judgment is based on the light that people have. He will not hold them accountable to a message about Christ which they never received.

People will be judged according to the revelation they have been given and the moral standard they acknowledged. Responsibility is proportionate to revelation, and God knows exactly how much revelation a person received and exactly how he or she responded to it. Just as there are different degrees of responsibility, so there are evidently different degrees of punishment for those who chose to reject the revelation they had been given (see Matt. 11:21-24; Luke 12:47-48; Heb. 2:2-3). "And from everyone who has been given much shall much be required" (Luke 12:48).

How much light do people who do not know about Christ really have? According to the Scriptures, they are not in total darkness about God, sin, or even salvation.

Ignorance of God. Underlying the objection about the heathen is the frequent assumption that they are completely ignorant of God and therefore innocent or unaccountable. This assumption is unfounded because their ignorance is only relative, not absolute. Paul's powerful exposé of man's rebellion against the one true God in Romans 1:18-25 is the central biblical text on this issue. Verse 20 describes the *external revelation* of God to all mankind: "For since the creation of the world His invisible attributes, His eternal power and divine nature, have been clearly seen, being understood through what has been made, so that they are without excuse." The creation points beyond itself to the One who made it, and no one can plead ignorance of the Creator, because all people have access to this general revelation of God. (General revelation is the spiritual knowledge available to all people, while special revelation refers to God's more direct means of communication to some people through dreams, visions, angels, and especially the Bible.)

The universe manifests God's "invisible attributes," including His "eternal power and divine nature." God's eternality, omnipotence, omniscience, and wisdom are "clearly seen" in creation, but because of their unrighteousness, men have suppressed these evident truths about God (Rom. 1:18). This revelation of God in nature is also affirmed by Psalm 19: "The heavens are telling of the glory of God; and their expanse is declaring the work of His hands. Day to day pours forth speech, and night to night reveals knowledge" (vv. 1-2). Paul told the residents of Lystra that in His creation God "did not leave Himself without witness" (Acts 14:15-17).

God has revealed Himself to all people not only externally in nature but also through *internal revelation:* "That which is known about God is evident within them; for God made it evident to them" (Rom. 1:19). Though fallen, humans are still "made in the likeness of God" (James 3:9) with a spiritual dimension and inner awareness of the existence of God. God "has also set eternity in their heart" (Ecc. 3:11), and it is "the fool" who suppresses this knowledge by saying in his heart, "There is no God" (Ps. 14:1). "For the wrath of God is revealed from heaven against all ungodliness and unrighteousness of men, who suppress the truth in unrighteousness" (Rom. 1:18).

There is a general revelation, therefore, of the existence and power of the eternal God to which people must respond. Those who reject or suppress the light they have been given are "without excuse" and under the wrath of the living God. They may never have heard about God the Son, but they have already rejected the truth that they know about God the Father.

At this point someone may respond, "What about the dedicated followers of other religions? Surely they are not rejecting the light they have about God." Once again, Romans 1 gives us an answer:

For even though they knew God, they did not honor Him as God, or give thanks; but they became futile in their speculations, and their foolish heart was darkened. Professing to be wise, they became fools, and exchanged the glory of the incorruptible God for an image in the form of corruptible man and of birds and four-footed animals and crawling creatures. Therefore God gave them over in the lusts of their hearts to impurity, that their bodies might be dishonored among them. For they exchanged the truth of God for a lie, and worshiped and served the creature rather than the Creator, who is blessed forever. Amen (Rom. 1:21-25).

Acording to Paul, the religions of man were spawned not out of a search for truth, but as a perversion of the truth that mankind originally had. Contrary to popular opinion, many religions did not evolve but devolved from a primal monotheism to a debased polytheism and animism. Because of unrighteousness, people quickly turned from a knowledge of God to their own futile speculations, "and their foolish heart was darkened." They substituted the creation for the Creator and developed their own ways of salvation.

It is significant that all non-Christian religions teach that salvation is achieved by human effort, ritual, sacrifice, and devotional service. These systems of salvation by works minimize two essential truths: the wretchedness of sin and the holiness of God. To be saved, a person must recognize his inability to atone for his own sins and cast himself on the mercy of the one true God. Jesus made it clear that human works will never bridge the moral gap between man and God; the only acceptable work is faith in Christ (John 6:28-29, 40).

There are truths in non-Christian religions because of general revelation, but there are also serious falsehoods in the critical areas of God, man, sin, and salvation due to a suppression of general revelation. Because of distortions like idolatry, those who participate in pagan religions actually compound their guilt by rejecting the external and internal revelation which they already have about the Creator.

Ignorance of sin. Romans 1 proclaims that people cannot plead ignorance of God the Father, though they may not have heard about God the Son. Romans 2 adds that all people also have an awareness of sin. They may not share the same set of moral principles, but everyone has *moral standards,* including the relativist. These standards emerge clearly whenever someone criticizes another. "Therefore you are without excuse, every man of you who passes judgment, for in that you judge another, you condemn yourself; for you who judge practice the same things" (Rom. 2:1).

Not only do we have moral standards, but we are all guilty of violating them. For instance, most people believe that consideration for the interests of others is preferable to selfishness, but how many consistently live up to this standard? Most husbands agree that they should treat their wives with kindness and respect, but what husband is perfect in his conformity to this principle?

Thus, when someone says, "If a person who does not know about Christ lives up to his own standard, he should not be judged," we can respond, "That sounds reasonable—if he flawlessly obeys his moral code, he should be considered innocent. But are there any people who do so?" Now and then someone may say, "Well, I have a friend who is a wonderful human being. He doesn't believe in God, and yet he is a caring, compassionate, and consistently helpful person." This will always be a third party, because others we know can sometimes maintain the appearance of living in conformity to their moral beliefs. But it is an exceedingly rare person who can say, "To the best of my knowledge, I have always kept my moral standards and never violated them."

People may try to minimize or rationalize sin, but they are not ignorant of it. They have a law inscribed in their hearts, and their *conscience* is aware of it:

> For when Gentiles who do not have the Law do instinctively the things of the Law, these, not having the Law, are a law to themselves, in that they show the work of the Law written in their hearts, their conscience bearing witness, and their thoughts alternately accusing or else defending them, on the day when, according to my Gospel, God will judge the secrets of men through Christ Jesus (Rom. 2:14-16).

One can sear his conscience (1 Tim. 4:2), but he cannot eliminate it. The conscience is a divinely given internal testimony to all people of their moral inadequacy. The first-century Roman philosopher Seneca wrote, "We are all wicked; what we blame in another each will find in his own bosom." The Roman poet Ovid confessed, "I see and approve the better course—I follow the worse." And the 18th-century English critic Samuel Johnson wisely observed, "Every man knows that of himself which he dare not tell his dearest friend."

The heathen, then, is not as ignorant as we might have thought. In his heart he is aware of the eternal and omnipotent Creator, and he knows about his own moral guilt. If he responds to these two truths rather than suppressing them, he will be moving in the direction of God's solution.

Ignorance of solution. Each person has some knowledge about God and sin for which he is accountable. This revelation requires a response, and, in this sense, everyone has a chance. God is aware of the light that each one has, and He knows the response of each human heart. We saw earlier that because He is fair, God will not hold anyone accountable for any knowledge he did not receive. But God is also holy and must judge those who do not respond to the truth they have. Salvation is a gift of God's grace—completely free; no one can earn or deserve it. God is therefore under no obligation to justify anyone, let alone those who fail to respond to the revelation they have received.

Every individual must shoulder his own burden of responsibility for making a decision about salvation. No one else can do this for him. There is a twofold revelation about God and sin, and the heathen's response should also be twofold: he must acknowledge his need (forgiveness of sin) and abandon himself to the mercy of the Creator (God). Both elements are found in Hebrews 11:6: "And without faith it is impossible to please Him, for he who comes to God must believe that He is, and that He is a rewarder of those who seek Him."

There is a God-shaped vacuum in every man; when a person recognizes his need for God and responds to the light he has received, God Himself will respond and reward that person with more light. There are a number of verses that affirm that those who seek God will find Him: "And you will seek Me and find Me, when you search for Me with all your heart" (Jer. 29:13). "Thou, O Lord, hast not forsaken those who seek Thee" (Ps. 9:10). "The Lord is near to all who call upon Him" (Ps. 145:18). "The Lord is good to those who wait for Him, to the person who seeks Him" (Lam. 3:25). David exhorted his son Solomon, "The Lord searches all hearts, and understands every intent of the thoughts. If you seek Him, He will let you find Him; but if you forsake Him, He will reject you forever" (1 Chron. 28:9; cf. 2 Chron. 15:2). Wisdom offered her treasures to those who would seek her: "I love those who love me; and those who diligently seek me will find me" (Prov. 8:17; also see Matt. 7:7-8).

Other verses tell us that God is actively involved on the other end of this process: "For the eyes of the Lord move to and fro throughout the earth that He may strongly support those whose heart is completely His" (2 Chron. 16:9). "For thus says the Lord God, 'Behold, I Myself will search for My sheep and seek them out'" (Ezek. 34:11). Jesus proclaimed, "For the Son of Man has come to seek and to save that which was lost" (Luke 19:10).

Seeking God is more than an intellectual process; it also involves a moral willingness:

> And this is the judgment, that the light is come into the world, and men loved the darkness rather than the light; for their deeds were evil. For everyone who does evil hates the light, and does not come to the light, lest his deeds should be exposed. But he who practices the truth comes to the light, that his deeds may be manifested as having been wrought in God (John 3:19-21).

John 7:17 also relates the moral dimension to the reception of spiritual truth: "If any man is willing to do His will, he shall know of the teaching, whether it is of God, or whether I speak from Myself." After his vision of the sheet, Peter came to understand that "God is not one to show partiality, but in every nation the man who fears Him and does what is right, is welcome to Him" (Acts 10:34-35; cf. 17:26-27).

On the other hand, David wrote that no one seeks after God or does good (Ps. 14:2-3) and Paul agreed (Rom. 3:10-12). Evidently, this means that no one pursues God with a whole heart or merits salvation by his works; apart from God's grace no one would seek Him. Yet we are still responsible. Those who respond positively to the light they have received will gain the knowledge that leads to salvation, and those who suppress it remain under the wrath of God. There is therefore no biblical warrant or need for a second chance.

God has seen fit to use His children as His primary means of providing additional light to those who want more. The New Testament strongly emphasizes the need for missions, so that all may be exposed to the Good News about Jesus.

> For there is no distinction between Jew and Greek; for the same Lord is Lord of all, abounding in riches for all who call upon Him; for "Whoever will call upon the name of the Lord will be saved." How then shall they call upon Him whom they have not heard? And how shall they hear without a preacher? And how shall they preach unless they are sent? Just as it is written, "How beautiful are the feet of those who bring glad tidings of good things!" (Rom. 10:12-15)

Missionaries must be sent so that people who have not heard may hear and believe. This was the point of Christ's Great Commission: "Go therefore and make disciples of all the nations, baptizing them in the name of the Father and the Son and the Holy Spirit, teaching them to observe all that I commanded you" (Matt. 28:19-20). Our Lord's last words prior to His ascension anticipated the spread of the Gospel throughout the whole world: "But you shall receive power when the Holy Spirit has come upon you; and you shall be My witnesses both in Jerusalem, and in all Judea and Samaria, and even to the remotest part of the earth" (Acts 1:8). After the Good News spread throughout Judea (Acts 1—7), it reached the Samaritans in Acts 8 through the ministry of Philip.

The incident with the Ethiopian eunuch (Acts 8:26-40) is a good illustration of God's provision of further light to a person who responds to the light he has received. The Ethiopian wanted to know more about the Suffering Servant of Isaiah 53, and God sent Philip to preach Jesus to him. A similar illustration appears in Acts 10 with the conversion of the Gentile centurion Cornelius and his household. Beginning in Acts 13, the missionary journeys of Paul and others carried the message of Jesus throughout the Roman Empire to Jews and Gentiles who needed to hear it.

There have been setbacks, but today this message has expanded in an unprecedented way all over the globe. Massive revivals have taken place in Africa, Indonesia, and other countries; millions have attended Christian rallies in South Korea; Gospel radio broadcasts reach all over the world through powerful transmitters; Christian organizations with global vision are reaching millions of people each week through newspapers, literature, films, and distribution of food and supplies. (These facts have led some people to turn our question around—"What about the heathen in the United States?")

In spite of all this, however, huge numbers of people have never heard about Jesus Christ. This is a major problem because of the significance of the name of Jesus, according to such passages as John 3:18; Acts 4:12; 5:41; Philippians 2:10; 1 John 3:23; 5:13; 3 John 7. (These verses refer, of course, to the *person* of Jesus and not the actual spelling in Greek of the name *Iesous.*) The resolution of this problem is found in the knowledge and power of God. He knows what is in everyone's heart, and He is capable of getting the word of salvation to all who want it.

Too often we think of God in Lilliputian terms. He is not an elderly gentleman looking down on earth from a celestial perch, biting His fingernails and saying, "I hope that missionary makes it. I hope he gets there in time!" If He really is the omniscient and omnipotent Creator and Sustainer of the universe, the Lord can get the message through, no matter where a person is (cf. Ps. 139:7-12). We cannot put Him in a box and limit the ways He might use to do this. Deuteronomy 29:29 tells us that "the secret things belong to the Lord our God." We know only a tiny part of the story.

The Bible repeatedly tells us that God can speak directly to the human heart. Consider, for example, the call of Abraham (Gen. 12:1-3), the story of Melchizedek (Gen. 14:18-20), Abimelech's dream in

Genesis 20:3, the Mesopotamian prophet Balaam (Num. 22—24), Nebuchadnezzar's dream in Daniel 2, God's warning to the Magi in Matthew 2:12, and Christ's appearance to the Pharisee Saul in Acts 9. Missionaries sometimes report stories of similar divine encounters today as well as unusual circumstances, obviously engineered by God to lead people into a knowledge of Christ.

A missionary to South Thailand wrote in a prayer letter to one of her supporting churches about a Muslim village leader who was directed in a dream to come to a missionary hospital to learn about Jesus and believe in Him. During that very week a missionary doctor who had worked in the Middle East for years made an unannounced visit to the same hospital. Because this doctor spoke fluent Arabic, he was able to share Christ with this Muslim.

Another story concerns a young man who started out on a quest for spiritual enlightenment in 1968. After a series of upsetting experiences with drugs, he found himself disoriented, wandering around the country. In Oregon he got involved with some Christians in a house ministry who shared the Gospel with him. Thinking he had become a Christian, he moved on and began to study any religion that mentioned Jesus. This opened him up to other religions and finally to Eastern mysticism and occultism. He spent four years in a Colorado monastery trying to develop his psychic powers. In one of his visions, he was impelled to find a spiritual master who was calling him. Convinced that this guru was in the Himalayan Mountains of Tibet, he proceeded on an arduous journey. Traveling the last 200 miles on foot at the tail end of the monsoon season, he stopped at one Buddhist monastery after another seeking his master. When he got above the tree line and reached an altitude between 14,000 and 15,000 feet, he was overwhelmed by a hunger for reality and cried out to God to know the truth. Suddenly he was stunned by the presence of Jesus Christ, and immediately became aware that the message he had heard five years earlier in Oregon was the truth. There, in the midst of the Himalayas, he trusted in Jesus as his true Master and Redeemer.

An incident that took place in 19th-century India illustrates the effective power of even a tiny fragment of God's Word. A caravan was crossing from one part of India to another and a missionary was traveling with it. As it passed along, a Hindu was so overcome by heat and weariness that he sank down, and was left to perish on the road. The missionary saw him, and kneeling by his side when the other travelers had passed on, whispered into his ear, "Brother, what is your hope?" The dying man raised himself a little, and with his last effort gasped out, "The blood of Jesus Christ His Son cleanseth from all sin." The astonished missionary wondered how this man, to all appearance a heathen, came to know Christ. Then he noticed a piece of paper grasped tightly in the dead man's hand. To his delight he saw it was a single leaf from the Bible containing the first chapter of John's first epistle, in which these words appear. On that single page this Hindu had found eternal life.

The Spirit of God uses the Word of God through men and women of God to make the message about the Son of God available to all who want to know the truth. There is no limit to the creative ways God can use to bring about this process.

But some people are troubled about those who lived before Christ. How could any of them have come to a knowledge of the true God? The answer to this problem is that the basis of salvation has always been the sacrifical death, burial, and resurrection of Christ Jesus. Though the saving work of Christ was future, God saw it from before the foundation of the earth. Not bound by time, the Lord applied the benefits of the death of Christ to all who called upon God for salvation. The means of salvation has always been faith, not works. The Old Testament clearly teaches that man is sinful and in need of God's grace (Isa. 59:2; 64:6; Ps. 6:1-2; 51:1-13).Thus, an Israelite needed to acknowledge his sin and turn to God in repentance and faith. The blood of the animal sacrifices did not save, but pointed ahead to the sacrifice of God's Son. In Old Testament times, people did not clearly understand this; like Abraham (Gen. 15:6), they were justified by grace through faith, and the object of that faith was God. But with the progressive revelation of the New Testament, the content of faith now includes the finished work of Christ.

The Old Testament also offers a few examples of Gentiles who came to know the one true God. These include Rahab the harlot (Josh. 2:1-21; Heb. 11:31), Ruth (Ruth 1:15-17), Naaman the Syrian (2 Kings 5:1-19), and the Ninevites who repented at the preaching of Jonah (Jonah 3:5-10).

Another problem associated with this question concerns infants and those who are mentally incapable of understanding the Gospel. Although the Bible is not explicit on this issue, it does provide certain principles and examples which suggest that God does not hold accountable those who do not have the capacity to make a decision about Him. Numbers 14:29 says that those who were under 20 would be spared the judgment of death in the wilderness. The younger generation was not held accountable for the sins of their fathers. Instead, they would be allowed to take possession of Canaan: "Moreover, your little ones who you said would become a prey, and your sons, who this day have no knowledge of good or evil, shall enter there, and I will give it to them, and they shall possess it" (Deut. 1:39). They had not reached the point where they were responsible for the knowledge of good or evil.

The issue here is the same one that runs throughout this chapter—the fairness of God. It is evident that God will be fair to those who are incapable of making an intellectual and moral response to Him.

The doctrine of infant salvation cannot be proved from the Bible, but there are some passages that imply that infants are in some special way kept by the power of God. Christ's teaching in Matthew 18:3-14 and 19:14 points in this direction:

> See that you do not despise one of these little ones, for I say to you, that their angels in heaven continually behold the face of My Father who is in heaven.... Thus it is not the will of your Father who is in heaven that one of these little ones perish.... Let the children alone, and do not hinder them from coming to Me; for the kingdom of heaven belongs to such as these (Matt. 18:10, 14; 19:14).

King David, after the loss of the infant born out of his adultery with Bathsheba, said, "But now he has died; why should I fast? Can I bring him back again? I shall go to him, but he will not return to me" (2 Sam. 12:23). Though David sinned, he knew the child would be with God, and he anticipated seeing him again.

Some people also look at Revelation 5:9 ("For Thou wast slain, and didst purchase for God with Thy blood men from every tribe and tongue and people and nation") as a partial reference to infant salvation. The argument is that this could account for the salvation of people in every tribe and nation that existed. If infants are covered by the atoning work of Christ, it is likely that these people will constitute a large percentage of the redeemed in heaven. (It is possible that this verse offers a partial solution to the problem of the American Indians before Columbus and other large groups unreached by missionaries.)

The second option to this question is shown in Chart 44.

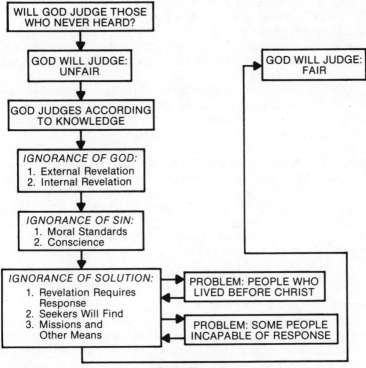

(CHART 44)

Third Option: God's Judgment of Those Who Have Not Heard Is Fair

When a person realizes that God's judgment is fair, it is time to personalize this question to show how it applies to him or her. We said that God judges according to the knowledge each individual has received and does not hold people accountable for what they could not know. But the other side of the coin is that God *does* hold us accountable for the knowledge we have received, and the person who asked this question is already aware of the message of the Gospel. Therefore, the real issue for him is no longer the heathen but himself. So we must ask, "What are *you* going to do with Jesus Christ?"

The heathen question cannot be used as a dodge to avoid a decision about Christ. Those who have heard the Gospel and rejected it are doubly guilty—they have rejected not only the Father but also the Son. And the Scriptures are clear about the judgment which awaits those who have refused God's offer of salvation. The wrath of God abides on them (John 3:36; cf. Heb. 2:3; 10:26-31).

Even those who have not heard about Christ have some knowledge about God, sin, and the solution of casting oneself upon the mercy of the one true God. This knowledge from general revelation is not contradicted but completed by special revelation.

Knowledge of God. The Scriptures reveal His character most clearly in the person of Jesus Christ (cf. John 1:14, 18).

Knowledge of sin. God's standard is perfection (Matt. 5:20, 48), and all of us fall short of that standard (Rom. 3:23). Apart from Christ, we are under the condemnation of God (Rom. 3:9; 6:23).

Knowledge of solution. God has provided a solution for sin through the work of His Son. We must acknowledge our need for His gift of righteousness and receive that gift by a choice of faith (Luke 19:10; John 1:12; 3:16; 14:6; 2 Cor. 5:21; 1 Peter 3:18).

Chart 45 shows the third option.

Summary and Flow Chart

When a person comes to understand Christ's claim to be the only way to the Father, he will probably wonder what happens to those who never heard about Jesus Christ. Some avoid the problem by claiming that these people will not be judged. That would solve the problem (and eliminate the need for missions), but it is not a viable option. The Bible repeatedly teaches the universality of sin and the judgment that sin produces. We must all stand before the holy God in final judgment.

This may seem unfair until we understand certain biblical principles about the justice of God and the knowledge of the heathen. God's justice is perfect, and it is based on the amount of light that each person has received. No one is entirely ignorant about the Creator, because, even apart from the special revelation of His Word, He has made himself known to all through general revelation. This includes His external revelation through the creation and His internal revelation in the human heart.

Nor is anyone completely ignorant about the problem of sin. We all

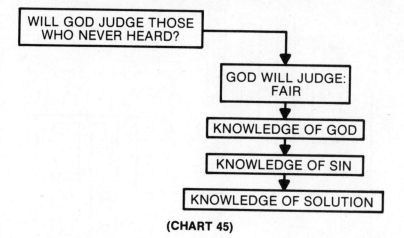

(CHART 45)

have moral standards that we cannot consistently maintain, and our conscience tells us of our moral inadequacy. This revelation about God and sin requires a response, and those who acknowledge their need and appeal to God for the answer will receive further light. God uses His children to carry the Good News about Christ to all parts of the world where people are seeking the one true God.

The basis of salvation in all ages has been the same—the redemptive work of Christ. The means of salvation has always been grace through faith. The content of this faith in the case of those who lived before Christ was not as specific as it is now because of progressive revelation. It is evident that infants and the mentally impaired are not held accountable to make a response they are incapable of making.

Those who ask this question must realize that, when they stand before God, the question will not be, "What about those who haven't heard?" but, "You heard the truth about Jesus Christ. How did you respond to Him?"

Supplemental Reading
(1) J. N. D. Anderson, *Christianity and Comparative Religion* (Tyndale). Chapter 5 offers excellent insights on this problem.

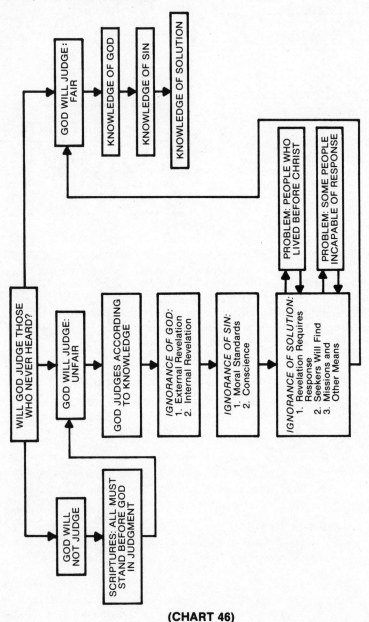

(CHART 46)

(2) David A. DeWitt, *Answering the Tough Ones* (Moody). Chapter 6 illustrates some ways of responding to this question.

(3) Norman L. Geisler, *The Roots of Evil* (Zondervan). Appendix 1 treats this issue succinctly.

(4) Gordon R. Lewis, *Judge for Yourself* (InterVarsity Press). Chapter 2 provides Scriptures and questions to help the reader think through this problem inductively.

(5) Paul E. Little, *How to Give Away Your Faith* (InterVarsity Press). Chapter 5 includes a helpful survey of how to handle this objection.

(6) Josh McDowell and Don Stewart, *Answers to Tough Questions* (Here's Life). See pages 129-32.

(7) Don Richardson, *Eternity in Their Hearts* (Regal Books). This absorbing book explores the almost universal concept of a supreme God in "primitive" and advanced cultures.

(8) R. C. Sproul, *Objections Answered* (Regal Books). See chapter 3 for a fine presentation of the answers to this question.

(9) Barry Wood, *Questions Non-Christians Ask* (Revell). Chapter 12 contains some good principles.

10

If Christianity Is True, Why Are There So Many Hypocrites?

Often-Asked Questions:

Too many Christians I know are phonies. If that's what Christianity is all about, why should I become a Christian?

If Christians are really concerned about others, why don't they show it?

Some non-Christians I know seem to live better lives than a lot of people who go to church—doesn't this show that Christianity isn't all it claims to be?

How can people who profess to be Christians still be full of racial hatred, materialism, and social insensitivity?

Many churchgoers seem to have holier-than-thou attitudes. Why should I join the ranks of the self-righteous?

Two Options

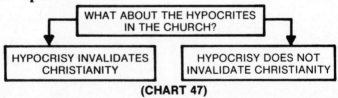

(CHART 47)

The real issue in this question is not merely the problem of profession versus practice. It is the implication that since Christians fall short, the truth claims of Christianity must also fall short. Does hypocritical behavior among those who profess to be Christians nullify the message about Christ? Some who have been disillusioned by the behavior of believers assume that it does, and they want no part of Christianity. The other possibility is that the truth of Christianity is not determined by the track record of adherents. (See Chart 47.)

First Option: Hypocrisy Invalidates Christianity

Where the Christian church has spread, it has resulted in incalculable benefits for millions of people on every level—spiritual, social, intellectual, physical. But people have a way of concentrating on the worst things about an individual or an institution, and so it is with the church. Many actually delight in rehearsing the worst travesties perpetrated in the name of Christianity; for example, the Crusades, the Spanish Inquisition, or the Salem witch trials. They also turn to the present and point to examples of financial exploitation, adultery, and other forms of unethical behavior among church leaders. They conclude, therefore, that the entire church is full of all sorts of hypocrites, and they imply that Christianity is not true because it does not work.

Forms of hypocrisy. Though we cannot agree that the church is *full* of hypocrites, we must acknowledge that there are some. We can't deny the abuses and inconsistencies mentioned above, and we should quickly admit that the church is not immune to this problem. In his *Pensees,* Blaise Pascal wrote, "Men never do evil so completely and cheerfully as when they do it from religious conviction." This is too often true, and hypocrisy has many sources and forms.

Some people become church members for social, business, and family reasons. They make a charade of faith and go through the religious motions once a week, but the spiritual reality in their lives is nil.

Even genuine believers fall prey to the pretense of being more righteous than they are. A yearning for acceptance can cause Christians to put on a facade of spirituality for fear that their Christian friends would reject them if they were more honest about their lives. Others become hypocritical in their behavior because they want to impress people and become the center of attention (e.g., Matt. 6:1-5).

Another form of hypocrisy is a greater love for orthodox doctrine about God, Christ, the Holy Spirit, and the Bible than for the objects of that doctrine.

There is also a great temptation among clergymen to maintain a superspiritual image in front of their congregations. But no minister can perfectly practice what he preaches. When ministers acknowledge this, they reduce the risk of hypocrisy. The problem arises when they convey the impression that they always live up to their sermons.

Yet another form of hypocrisy occurs when Christians make solemn public vows and flagrantly violate them. Vows of marriage and church membership, which are supposed to be declarations of commitment, are later voided out of convenience.

Hypocrisy, then, is a reality that has not been rooted out of the Christian church. But it would be wrong to condemn all Christians as hypocrites just as it would be wrong to condemn the medical profession because of wrong diagnoses and ineffective treatments, as well as certain instances of malpractice. For every example of hypocrisy in the church, counter-examples of genuinely transformed lives can be multiplied.

Definition of hypocrisy. In ancient Greece, the word *hypokrisis* referred to a "pretense" or an "outward show." Another word, *hypokrites,* meant "hypocrite, pretender, dissembler," and was originally used to describe Greek actors who spoke through masks (the kind sometimes found on playbills and theater decorations) during their performances. Thus, the word came to be used of a person who was pretending to be something he was not. The hypocrite is living a lie because he makes a pretense of moral character that he does not possess. He carefully covers his faults so that others will have a higher opinion of him.

Thus, for a person to come to Christ on His terms, he must become the opposite of a hypocrite. That is, he must acknowledge his own lack of merit in God's sight and accept the unmerited favor (grace) that God has provided in His gift of Christ's righteousness to those who come to Him. Before a person can embrace Christ as Saviour, he must admit that he is a sinner. Jesus told the Pharisees, "It is not those who are healthy who need a physician, but those who are sick; I did not come to call the righteous, but sinners" (Mark 2:17). It is the man who thinks he is morally healthy before God apart from Christ who is the real hypocrite, because he considers himself righteous when he is in fact a transgressor of God's moral law. "If we say that we have no sin, we are deceiving ourselves, and the truth is not in us. . . . If we say that we have not sinned, we make Him a liar, and His Word is not in us" (1 John 1:8, 10).

False assumptions. Three false assumptions are associated with this objection concerning the hypocrites, and they need to be exposed as such before the objection can be overcome. The *first false assumption* is that *profession means possession.* Many people take it for granted that whoever claims to be a Christian must therefore be a Christian. But there is a great deal of difference between Christianity and "churchianity"; many church members are not members of the body of Christ. Being religious is not synonymous with having a relationship. The Pharisees were highly religious, but many of them did not know God. Profession does not mean possession.

When this objection about the hypocrites surfaces, it is important to be sure we are talking about real Christians—that is, those who have admitted their sinfulness and turned to Christ as their Saviour. Anything of genuine value like money, jewels, and art can and will be counterfeited. But the fact that counterfeit money exists does not mean we should stop using money. Similarly, reproductions or forgeries of great paintings do not lessen the value of the genuine paintings. Church attendance, high moral standards, and religious profession do not make someone a biblical Christian any more than going to a ballpark makes a person a baseball player. This can help alleviate the problem raised by the hypocrite question, because many of the misdeeds associated with Christianity are not accomplished by genuine Christians.

The *second false assumption* is that *Christians claim to be perfect.* Some non-Christians put Christians in a lose-lose situation. On the one hand, they impose a double standard, expecting Christians to behave on a level that they themselves never think of attaining. On the other hand, they are offended by righteous behavior because of their inward sense of guilt. When their Christian friends behave in a godly manner, they assume it must be a show and equate piety with pretense.

But ethical behavior does not have to mean self-righteousness; one can be moral without being moralistic. In fact, a true Christian should be the first to admit that he is not perfect in his practice. Christians do not claim to be sinless, but they do claim to be perfectly forgiven.

It is clear from such passages as Romans 7:14-25; Galatians 5:13-26; Philippians 3:12-16; and 1 John 1:5-10 that Christians have not arrived at a state of complete Christlikeness. Until we see Christ "just as He is" (1 John 3:2) and become like Him, no believer will be immune to the pull of various kinds of sins. We will fail, but this does not invalidate Christianity; it simply means that for a time we withdraw from our walk with Christ.

Thus, the real issue is not perfection but progression. The quality of a Christian's life will fluctuate, but over a period of time it should progress toward increasing Christlikeness. Unlike the hypocrite, this change is not an external veneer but is being wrought from the inside out.

So it is unwise to compare the life of one believer with the lives of others. It is more valid to compare what he is now with what he was before coming to Christ. If we met someone on the beach with an average physique who proudly told us about the terrific exercise program he has been following, we wouldn't be terribly impressed. But if we found out that he had been a 97-pound weakling only six weeks before, our assessment of his exercise program would suddenly change. Similarly, some non-Christians are better adjusted people than some Christians, but this does not mean that Christianity is ineffective. Non-Christians may point to inconsistencies in the lives of Christians they know, especially new believers. But if they take a closer look, they will probably find that some real changes have actually taken place when they compare the believer's present life with what it used to be before he became a Christian.

Even though the Spirit of God indwells and empowers believers, it is only too easy for us to "quench the Spirit" (1 Thes. 5:19) and grieve Him (Isa. 63:10; Eph. 4:30). When a true Christian fails to progress in his faith and leads a life of inconsistency or hypocrisy, he will begin to experience the firm but loving discipline of his heavenly Father. "God deals with you as with sons; for what son is there whom his father does not discipline? But if you are without discipline, of which all have become partakers, then you are illegitimate children and not sons" (Heb. 12:7-8). Because God loves His children, "He disciplines us for our good, that we may share His holiness" (Heb. 12:10). This divine training is designed to yield "the peaceful fruit of righteousness" (Heb. 12:11) which will attract others to Christianity rather than repel them.

The *third false assumption* is that *all sin is hypocrisy*. If this were true, a Christian who openly acknowledges that his behavior is far from perfect would nevertheless become a hypocrite every time he sins. It is much more reasonable to say that while all hypocrisy is sin, not all sin is hypocrisy. Sin is a general term, and hypocrisy, like theft and slander, is a particular species of sin. Thus, while all Christians sin (1 John 1:8, 10), not all Christians are hypocrites.

Christ's view of hypocrisy. Only Christ used the word *hypocrite* in the New Testament, and He reserved His harshest words for those who fell into this category. Matthew 23 contains a frightening series of woes delivered by our Lord to the religious leaders of His day (the scribes and Pharisees) who made an outward display of godliness but inwardly did not know God. They took pride in their knowledge of the Law and the rituals, but God's Law was not written on their hearts. In their pomp and formalism, they sought the plaudits of men rather than the approval of God. Their self-righteousness prevented them from seeing their own sin. This is why Jesus told them, "You are like whitewashed tombs which on the outside appear beautiful, but inside they are full of dead men's bones and all uncleanness. Even so you too outwardly appear righteous to men, but inwardly you are full of hypocrisy and lawlessness" (Matt. 23:27-28).

Today, also, there are religious pretenders in the church who are fooling others, and just as tragically, fooling themselves. But God, who searches men's hearts, cannot be deceived and will one day tell these modern-day Pharisees the awful words, "I never knew you; depart from Me, you who practice lawlessness" (Matt. 7:23).

Christ uttered these stern words not only because of the self-deceiving pride involved in such hypocrisy but also because of the great damage that hypocrisy causes. When religious fraud is exposed in the lives of ministers, many people become disillusioned and disappointed. Hypocrisy causes people to stumble, and the effects can be far-reaching.

Not only is Jesus adamantly opposed to hypocrisy in all its forms but so is the entire Bible. The prophets of the Old Testament continually denounced religious orthodoxy and formalism that lacked inner reality. The Lord denounced Judah through the Prophet Isaiah saying, "This people draw near with their words and honor Me with their lip service, but they remove their hearts far from Me, and their reverence for Me consists of tradition learned by rote" (Isa.

29:13; also see Prov. 26:23-26; Isa. 1:13-17; Jer. 7:8-10; 9:8). Amos made this point abundantly clear in his oracle to the Northern Kingdom of Israel:

> I hate, I reject your festivals, nor do I delight in your solemn assemblies. Even though you offer up to Me burnt offerings and your grain offerings, I will not accept them; and I will not even look at the peace offerings of your fatlings. Take away from Me the noise of your songs; I will not even listen to the sound of your harps. But let justice roll down like waters and righteousness like an ever-flowing stream (Amos 5:21-24).

New Testament authors are also united in their opposition to religious hypocrisy and pretense. Paul describes certain people as "holding to a form of godliness, although they have denied its power; avoid such men as these" (2 Tim. 3:5). Writing to his co-worker Titus, Paul says, "They profess to know God, but by their deeds they deny Him, being detestable and disobedient, and worthless for any good deed" (Titus 1:16; also see Rom. 2:1, 3, 17-29; Gal. 2:11-14; 1 Tim. 4:1-2; James 1:22-26; 2:14-26; 2 Peter 2:17, 19; 1 John 1:6; 4:20; Jude 12-13; Rev. 2:9).

So the non-Christian who is opposed to religious hypocrisy actually agrees with Christ and the Bible on this point.

The first option to this question is seen in Chart 48.

Second Option: Hypocrisy Does Not Invalidate Christianity

Christians do not claim to be perfect, but they do claim to be forgiven by the One who is perfect, Jesus Christ. Because of human frailty, inconsistency, and rebellion against God, the performance of the Christian church through the centuries has been far from ideal. But Christianity really stands or falls on the person of Christ, not the performance of Christians. If Christ was a hypocrite, the whole structure of Christianity crumbles into a heap.

The officers who were sent out by the chief priests and the Pharisees to seize Jesus returned empty-handed and said of Him, "Never did a man speak the way this Man speaks" (John 7:46). Jesus spoke the noblest words ever spoken, and the standards He raised were so high that they were humanly unattainable. But in the life of Jesus, His words and works were a seamless piece; His precepts were

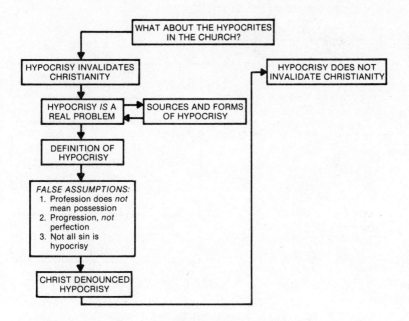

(CHART 48)

perfectly matched by His practice. He spoke of loving one another and displayed unmatched compassion for people on every level. He spoke of servanthood and became the model of servanthood. He spoke of obedience to the will of His Father and walked every moment in complete dependence and submission to the life and will of God. He was the humblest and wisest man who ever lived, and in His character, He perfectly realized the fruit of the Spirit: love, joy, peace, patience, kindness, goodness, faithfulness, gentleness, self-control. He spoke the truth and lived the truth, and when He publicly asked, "Which one of you convicts me of sin?" no one was able to respond. His own disciples who lived with Him day and night for more than three years declared Him to be sinless (1 Peter 2:22; 1 John 3:5).

Jesus was against hypocrisy, and His life was the antithesis of

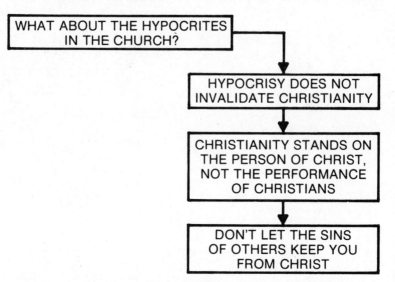

(CHART 49)

hypocrisy. Our job is to help those who raise the question of hypocrisy see that they actually agree with us and with Jesus on this issue. We need to tell them, "Christ strongly denounced the hypocrites of His day and was the opposite of a hypocrite in His own life and character. Why should you let these people come between you and Christ?" No one ought to miss out on a relationship with Jesus because of someone else's inconsistency and hypocrisy. He offers His perfect righteousness to imperfect people who repent and turn to Him. It would be foolish to let resentment against hypocritical behavior prevent you from receiving this priceless gift. Christ said that the religious hypocrites will not "escape the sentence of hell" (Matt. 23:33). Why plan to spend an eternity with them by rejecting Christ?

Sometimes the issue of hypocrisy is raised as an excuse for rejecting Christianity or as a dodge for avoiding a confrontation with the claims of Christ. When this happens, the objector should be brought as quickly as possible to the realization that the real issue is not the performance of Christians but the person of Christ. Religious

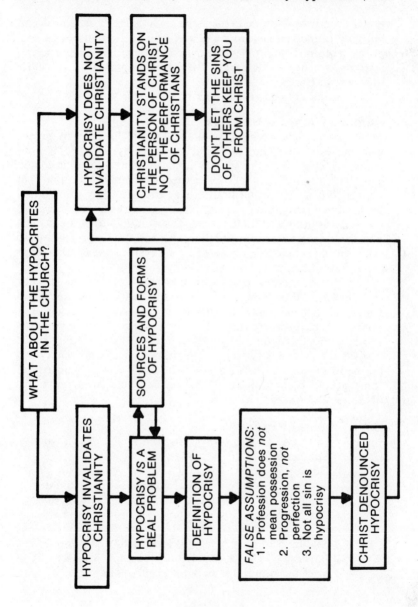

(CHART 50)

pretense and abuses done in the name of Christianity are a problem, but they cannot be blamed on Christ or used to avoid one's own problem of sin. That problem needs to be dealt with whether a person is troubled by hypocrites or not. The only solution to that problem is the work of Christ.

The second option to the hypocrite question is shown in Chart 49.

Summary and Flow Chart

Many people have been disappointed and disillusioned by people who profess to be Christians but live ungodly lives. Some non-Christians claim that Christianity cannot be true because it doesn't work—the church is full of hypocrites. There is no question that hypocrisy is a real problem and that there are many sources and forms of hypocrisy. But on closer examination, the hypocrisy issue is not as devastating as it first appears. The word *hypocrite* applies to a person who pretends to be something he is not. But the prerequisite to becoming a genuine Christian is an open acknowledgment that one is sinful, not righteous.

In addition, we must correct three false assumptions to alleviate this objection: First, not all who profess to be Christians are in fact Christians. Second, real Christians do not claim to live perfect lives. Third, though believers sin, not all sin is hypocrisy. Furthermore, Christ Himself denounced hypocrisy, and so does the entire Bible. Christ's character was perfect, and this is the basis of Christianity, not the performance of Christians. We shouldn't let the hypocrisy of some people become a barrier between the one who raises this objection and Christ.

Supplemental Reading

(1) David A. DeWitt, *Answering the Tough Ones* (Moody). See chapter 10.

(2) Gordon R. Lewis, *Judge for Yourself* (InterVarsity Press). Chapter 5 develops the options and offers a number of biblical texts that will aid the reader in thinking through this objection.

(3) R. C. Sproul, *Objections Answered* (Regal Books). See chapter 5 for a very helpful presentation of this problem.

(4) Barry Wood, *Questions Non-Christians Ask* (Revell). A brief but useful discussion is given in chapter 5.

11
What About Good Works?

Often-Asked Questions:
> *If people try their very best, won't God let them into heaven?*
> *I know many non-Christians who are far better people than most of the Christians I've met. Would God really refuse them?*
> *Doesn't God require me only to be better than the average human?*
> *Don't I have to have faith in Christ and live a good life if I want to go to heaven?*

Two Options

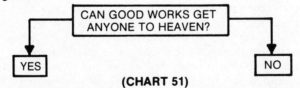

(CHART 51)

The options for this question are quite straightforward. The first option holds that good works play an integral, if not the only, role in achieving heaven. The second option claims that salvation is attained solely through Christ's gift on our behalf. (See Chart 51.)

The biblical perspective on this question is significant. Ten of the eleven major religions of the world teach salvation by good deeds.

Christianity stands alone with its emphasis on grace rather than works for salvation.

First Option: Good Deeds Can Get Us to Heaven

Man has sought for millenniums to appease God by his own efforts. Knowing, however, that he could not achieve perfection, man devised various systems that called for degrees of goodness. He sought to elevate himself toward God by performing a certain number of good deeds. These systems appeal to many people, but, on close scrutiny, we find four major problems with them: they are arbitrary; they offer no assurance of salvation; they ask God to approve of evil; and they contradict the Bible.

(1) *They are arbitrary.* First, who determines which standard of works we should follow? Some would say we should follow the Ten Commandments. Others choose the Five Pillars of Islam and still more opt for the Golden Rule. Second, if we try to follow a system of works, how well do we have to do? What will be good enough for God to let us into heaven?

In a recent adult discussion group, someone asked, "What is good enough to get man to heaven?" Some people responded, "We must keep the Ten Commandments and follow the Golden Rule." The next question was, "How many keep those two things?" The answer: "Even though we don't keep them perfectly, we should all do our best." A third question immediately followed: "Do any of you do your best all the time?" No one could respond with a resounding yes, so the group lowered the standard again. They felt that if you tried your best *most* of the time, you could make it. But what does most of the time mean? Perhaps 51 percent? Or 85 percent? In the final round, the group admitted that it was unable to determine one level of commitment that would be necessary for salvation.

This becomes frustrating because we don't know how God grades our performance. Does He grade on a bell-shaped curve? Does He compare us against ourselves or against others? If it is against others, does He compare us with Jack the Ripper and the Boston Strangler or with Albert Schweitzer and Mother Theresa?

(2) *They offer no assurance of salvation.* Even though man's systems are very arbitrary, it is amazing how many people hope they will make it. It's as though we put the human race on a ladder. The more good deeds a person does, the higher on the rungs he goes, with

the lowest scoundrel on the bottom and the most saintly on the top. If we were to ask people to select the rung on which God would draw the line for salvation, most would respond that the cutoff point is just below *their* rung. But even though they might think they have made it, they have a nagging uncertainty. *They can't be sure.* Those who play a balancing scale game with their good versus their evil deeds cannot know the outcome until the end, when it is too late.

(3) *They ask God to approve of evil.* A system that demands less than perfection must allow some evil, and, therefore, must ask God to approve of this evil. If God allowed imperfect people into heaven, then heaven would no longer be perfect. Heaven is without suffering and sin, not just a place where there is minimal suffering and sin (Rev. 21—22). If you had a glass of 100 percent pure water and you added just a speck of dirt, the water would no longer be pure. The same idea is true of heaven.

Some have argued that heaven would be all right if God would permit basically good people to enter. Even if it wouldn't be perfect, it would be enjoyable. But God reminds us that He once wiped out all evil except for some basically good people—Noah and his family. But the world's condition did not stay good; it quickly became much worse.

This is why God must eradicate sin from His kingdom, for heaven would soon look like earth if imperfect people were allowed in. God cannot approve of any evil. His flawless character demands that He judge all evil. God says that anyone less than perfect must be separated from Him (Isa. 59:2).

Take note that the topic of reincarnation sometimes comes to the surface here. The reincarnationist believes that good deeds will get one to a perfect state, but only after a long series of transmigrations. After millions of lives, one can attain perfection, and thus become acceptable to God. We will deal more fully with reincarnation in the appendix to this chapter.

(4) *They contradict the Bible.* Any system of salvation by works clearly conflicts with the Bible. The Scriptures plainly teach that the only way to overcome the gap between God and man is through faith in Christ, not good works.

> Because by the works of the Law no flesh will be justified in His sight; for through the Law comes the knowledge of sin (Rom. 3:20).

> Now to the one who works, his wage is not reckoned as a favor, but what is due. But to the one who does not work, but believes in Him who justifies the ungodly, his faith is reckoned as righteousness (Rom. 4:4-5).

> Now that no one is justified by the Law before God is evident; for, "The righteous man shall live by faith" (Gal. 3:11).

> He saved us, not on the basis of deeds which we have done in righteousness, but according to His mercy, by the washing of regeneration and renewing by the Holy Spirit (Titus 3:5).

The whole works system is rooted in the subtle sin of pride. Pride caused Satan and Adam to fall, and pride continues to keep man away from God's solution. By following a works system, man seeks to give credit to himself. If he trusts in Christ, only God can receive credit. There are many reasons why God chose to save man by grace, but the one Paul mentions is related to man's pride:

> For by grace you have been saved through faith; and that not of yourselves, it is the gift of God; not as a result of works, that no one should boast (Eph. 2:8-9).

Some may question the testimony of the Bible, and at that juncture, we may need to go back and deal with the Bible's reliability.

If works are not the means of salvation, what is the answer? Before moving on to the second option, see Chart 52 for the first one.

Second Option: Good Deeds Cannot Get Us to Heaven

One of Christ's greatest discourses was the Sermon on the Mount where He gave God's standard for entering heaven: "Therefore you are to be perfect, as your heavenly Father is perfect" (Matt. 5:48). The standard is *perfection*. Note the qualifying phrase: "as your heavenly Father is perfect." He is holy and without blemish. Christ had already told the multitude that a perfection equal to that of their religious leaders would not be enough to save them: "For I say to you, that unless your righteousness surpasses that of the scribes and Pharisees, you shall not enter the kingdom of heaven" (Matt. 5:20).

We must go back in time and recreate the atmosphere of Israel

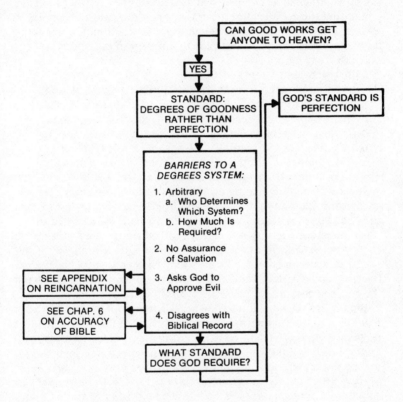

(CHART 52)

during the time of Christ. The religious leaders of the day had committed themselves to a good deeds system for salvation. The Pharisees had deceived themselves into believing that they had achieved perfection by observing their outward rituals. Christ exposed their sinful hearts by stating that God demanded perfection not only in their actions but also in their attitudes. They may not have committed the act of murder, but they had the attitude of murder in their hearts (Matt. 5:21-22). They may not have committed the act of adultery, but they had the attitude of adultery in their hearts (Matt. 5:27-28).

Christ went on to say:

> And if your right eye makes you stumble, tear it out, and throw it from you; for it is better for you that one of the parts of your body perish, than for your whole body to be thrown into hell. And if your right hand makes you stumble, cut it off, and throw it from you; for it is better for you that one of the parts of your body perish, than for your whole body to go into hell (Matt. 5:29-30).

Jesus was not advocating a new cult of self-mutilization. He was graphically illustrating a point. The Pharisees were trying to earn their salvation by their good deeds. Christ had just declared that it was not just their actions but also their attitudes that God considered. If they persisted down this foolish road of external religiosity and works in order to enter God's kingdom, then they must understand the cost. To be perfect, they would have to eliminate everything from their beings that would cause them to do evil.

But the problem remains. Even if they gouged out their eyes to keep from lusting, they could still have the attitude of lust. Christ made it quite clear that (1) salvation does not come to those who make an attempt at being perfect, but only to those who are perfect; and (2) man is imperfect, not only in his actions, but also in his attitudes.

How we illustrate man's imperfection is crucial, if we want to communicate the claims of Christ. When Christians think of man's sin, they think in *theological terms* and see all men's sin as equal. When the non-Christian considers sin and imperfection, he thinks in *sociological terms* and notices vast differences in the sins of men. Our friends must understand that we are not saying that they are the most vicious people alive when we talk of how short they fall of God's standard of perfection.

You may want to use a variation of the following illustration as an aid in communicating this truth. Imagine all of humanity lined up around the rim of the Grand Canyon. The object is for each person to jump from one side of the rim to the other. Each person's ability to jump is directly proportional to how many good deeds he has performed. The first person to jump is a mass murderer who goes only one foot and plummets downward. The average person can bound for 8 to 10 feet, but this too is still pitifully short of the goal. An exceptionally self-sacrificing humanitarian outdistances most of humanity by going 150 feet away from the bank. But the same thing occurs to everyone who jumps; each falls short of the other bank. There are great differences among people as to their levels of goodness, but all of mankind fall short of perfection.

Or, you can illustrate this concept as shown in Chart 53.

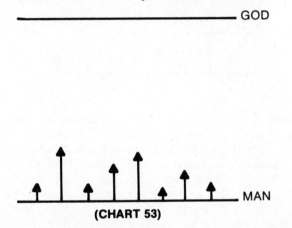

(CHART 53)

The person represented by the second arrow might be inclined to compare his life with the lives of those around him and think that God will surely let him into heaven because of the relative quality of his life. But the standard God requires is absolute, not relative. It is nothing less than the perfect life of Christ. God will not and cannot lower His standards of righteousness and grade on a curve.

To be more accurate, the upper line would actually be far higher than portrayed in this diagram. On that scale, the relative differences in human works pale into insignificance. (Similarly, if the earth could be reduced to the size of a basketball and held in your hands, your fingers would not be able to tell the difference between Mt. Everest and low-lying hills.)

This is why it was necessary for God to bridge the gap (see Chart 54).

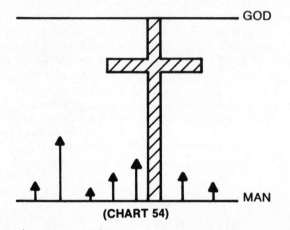

(CHART 54)

Paul tells us in Romans 3:23, "For all have sinned and fall short of the glory of God." This means that every human being is imperfect. Some people may not readily admit their lack of perfection, and when this happens, we introduce our 24-hour thought camera. We lightheartedly ask our friends if they would care to let us see all of their thoughts for the last 24 hours projected on the wall in living color. Then we remind them of Samuel Johnson's famous one-liner: "Every man knows that of himself which he dare not tell his dearest friend." It is important that we share with our friends that we don't want them to see our thoughts for the past 24 hours any more than they want us to see theirs. If not, this illustration could sound snobbish and self-righteous.

James tells us how little it takes to become imperfect: "For whoever keeps the whole Law and yet stumbles in one point, he has become guilty of all" (James 2:10). Suppose you were dangling by a chain from a 2,000-foot precipice and one of the links in the chain breaks. It doesn't matter whether just one link breaks or they all break. The result is the same—you plummet to your death. So it is when man violates God's Law, whether there are numerous transgressions or just one.

The justice of God demands that a penalty be paid for this disobedience. The judgment for sin is eternal separation from the holy God. Isaiah tells us that our sins caused us to be separated from God: "But your iniquities have made a separation between you and your God" (Isa. 59:2). Paul also describes the penalty in Romans 6:23: "For the wages of sin is death." God cannot change the penalty, for if He did, He would no longer be a just judge. The penalty must be paid. Either man pays his own penalty, or someone else pays it.

God's justice demands payment, and God's love offers us a substitute. Christ paid our debt on the cross of Calvary. "But God demonstrates His own love toward us, in that while we were yet sinners, Christ died for us" (Rom. 5:8). We can rejoice that Paul didn't stop Romans 6:23 half way through but finished the verse for us: "For the wages of sin is death, but the free gift of God is eternal life in Christ Jesus our Lord." Peter describes the beauty of Christ's sacrifice for us: "And He Himself bore our sins in His body on the cross, that we might die to sin and live to righteousness; for by His wounds you were healed" (1 Peter 2:24). "For Christ also died for sins once for all, the just for the unjust, in order that He might bring us to God, having been put to death in the flesh, but made alive in the spirit" (1 Peter 3:18).

Consider a story that depicts both the justice and love that God displayed to His creation. One day during the Great Depression, police hauled a frightened old man before the magistrate in a New York City night court. They charged him with petty larceny; he was starving and had stolen a loaf of bread. By coincidence, the mayor himself, Fiorello LaGuardia, was presiding over the court that night. LaGuardia sometimes sat in for judges as a way of keeping close to the citizens of the city. LaGuardia fined the old man $10. "The law is the law, and cannot be broken," the mayor pointed out. At the same time, he took a $10 bill out of his own wallet and told the man he would pay his fine for him. Then LaGuardia turned to the others in the courtroom and "cited" each of them for living in a city that did not reach out and help its poor and elderly, tempting them unduly to steal. The mayor fined everyone in the audience 50¢ each, passed around his famous fedora to collect the fines, and turned over its contents to the amazed defendant. The hat contained almost $50. The old man left the courtroom with tears in his eyes.

God provided a solution to our problem, and freely offers it to us as a gift. Christ's death paid for everyone's sin, but each individual must decide if he wants Christ's payment or if he plans to pay the debt himself. Each person must personally receive this gift, and when he does, the payment that it provides is credited to his account. God can then reckon that person's debt of sin as "PAID IN FULL." The need for receiving Christ personally is mentioned by John: "But as many as received Him, to them He gave the right to become children of God, even to those who believe in His name" (John 1:12). For a more detailed explanation of what is entailed in receiving Christ as Saviour, see chapter 13.

We solve our problem of separation from God by trusting in Christ's payment alone and not by seeking to pay the penalty with our own good deeds. While good works might make us better people, we will still fall far short of God's standard. Only through Christ can we be restored to a position of perfection before God. The moment we trust Christ, we appear as perfect before the Father. He no longer sees us in our sin but sees Christ in us.

One of the richest verses in Scripture can be used to illustrate this concept. Paul wrote: "He [God] made Him [Christ] who knew no sin to be sin on our behalf, that we might become the righteousness of God in Him" (2 Cor. 5:21). If I add up my own accomplishments in the flesh, they add up to sin (see Chart 55, left column); but if the accomplishments of Christ are added up, the sum is righteousness (right column).

Arrow 1 represents the first half of this verse (Christ placed our sin on His account), and arrow 2 represents the second half (Christ placed His righteousness on our account).

An illustration concerning a young boy and his balloon casts light on the matter. The boy went into the house one day, peered at his father through the orange balloon, and cried, "Daddy, Daddy! You're an orange daddy; you're an orange daddy!"

The father smiled, removed the balloon, and said to his son, "Now, what do you see?"

The boy responded, "Aw, now you're just an ordinary daddy."

He quickly pressed his face flush against the balloon again and excitedly declared, "You're an orange daddy again!" The father asked him why he appeared to be orange. "Because I'm looking at you

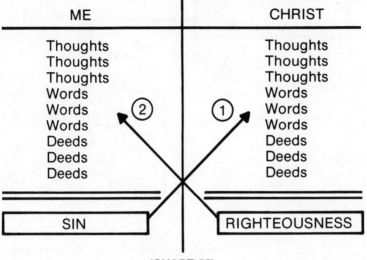

(CHART 55)

through my orange balloon," said the young boy.

When we belong to Christ, God views us differently in Him and sees perfect children. We call this *positional sanctification* (1 Cor. 6:11). In Christ, we become new creatures (2 Cor. 5:17). When we receive our resurrected bodies, we will be completely free from any blemish of sin (*ultimate sanctification;* Eph. 5:26-27).

Christ's disciples were immersed in a society caught up with a salvation by works mentality. Early in His ministry, people came to Christ and asked what they must do to work the works of God. Christ responded, "This is the work of God, that you believe in Him whom He has sent" (John 6:29). John 14:6 tells us that it is through Christ alone that salvation is possible. (If someone has problems with Christ's credentials, remember the case for His resurrection in the appendix to chapter 4.)

God will not accept our good deeds as payment for our sins. Even if we were 99 percent good, the one percent that was imperfect would be enough to disqualify us from heaven. In Ephesians 2:8-10, we learn how good works fit with salvation. Good works are not the *means* of salvation, they are the *result* of salvation. Having accepted Christ and

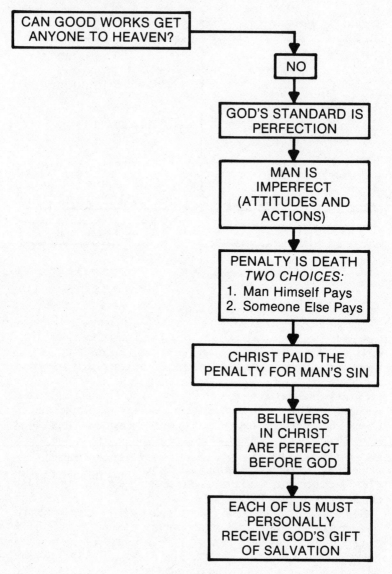

CAN GOOD WORKS GET ANYONE TO HEAVEN?

NO

GOD'S STANDARD IS PERFECTION

MAN IS IMPERFECT (ATTITUDES AND ACTIONS)

PENALTY IS DEATH
TWO CHOICES:
1. Man Himself Pays
2. Someone Else Pays

CHRIST PAID THE PENALTY FOR MAN'S SIN

BELIEVERS IN CHRIST ARE PERFECT BEFORE GOD

EACH OF US MUST PERSONALLY RECEIVE GOD'S GIFT OF SALVATION

(CHART 56)

His payment for us, we become children of God. As such, we seek to please Him and become involved in good works.

See Chart 56 for this option.

Summary and Flow Chart

We first considered the possibility of getting into heaven through good works. Most religious systems of works demand that we achieve certain degrees of goodness, since we cannot reach perfection. This appeals to many people raised in a society with a strong work ethic. But, for all its appeal, there are several barriers that render this option invalid:

(1) The different work systems are arbitrary. Who decides which one is right?

(2) We can never have assurance of salvation under a system of works. The standards change like shifting sands, and no one can be sure if his life is good enough.

(3) The good-deeds mentality is, in essence, asking God to approve of limited evil and assimilate it into His kingdom. (This relates to the question of reincarnation treated in the appendix to this chapter.) God is perfect, and He cannot "grade on a curve" by lowering His standard for salvation.

(4) Finally, any system of salvation by works stands in direct disagreement with the Scriptures.

So, if degrees of goodness are not the standard, what is? Christ has set the standard by being perfect Himself. Man is imperfect, and the result of sin is separation from God. There are only two choices for paying the penalty for sin: (1) we can pay the penalty ourselves, or (2) we can allow someone else to pay the price for us.

Christ has paid our penalty, but we must personally accept Christ's payment because He will not force it on us. Those who receive Christ's gift become perfect in the sight of God, and are reconciled to Him. Man cannot attain salvation by good deeds because the standard is perfection, and that is achievable only through Christ.

Supplemental Reading

(1) David A. DeWitt, *Answering the Tough Ones* (Moody). Chapter 9 has some good illustrations.

(2) Walter Martin, *The New Cults* (Vision House). Chapter 11 has a brief but articulate analysis of reincarnation.

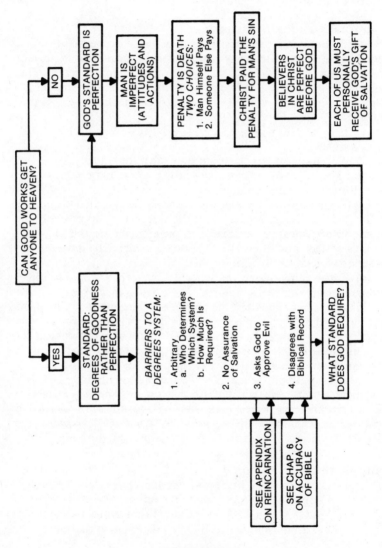

(CHART 57)

(3) Robert A. Morey, *Reincarnation and Christianity* (Bethany Fellowship). Exposes several logical inconsistencies in the system of reincarnation.
(4) R. C. Sproul, *Objections Answered* (Regal Books). Draws a good comparison between humanism and Christianity in chapter 6.
(5) Barry Wood, *Questions Non-Christians Ask* (Revell). Morality and spirituality are nicely distinguished in pages 43-49.

Appendix on Reincarnation

The theory of reincarnation may need to be examined when discussing the issue of good deeds as a means of getting to heaven. Reincarnation is the epitome of the salvation by works system.

The major tenet of all forms of reincarnation is a belief in a continuously rotating cycle of one's soul from body to body until it achieves a state of sinlessness. The soul passes from one life form to another at the point of death. In some versions the soul goes only into another human body, while other versions teach that the soul can pass into lower forms of life as well. Reincarnation, then, is a purification process whereby one attains salvation through his own merit and effort.

A person's progress through the cycles of life is determined by the law of karma. Karma is the moral law of cause and effect. A person's present fate, whether good or bad, is based on his actions in previous lives. This is the idea of reaping what you have sown. Sin cannot be forgiven but must be paid for by suffering in the next life. The reincarnationist believes that if we are suffering now, it is because of sins in our past life. The payment must be made by the individual who committed the sins, and it cannot be circumvented in any way. This system allows no room for grace or forgiveness.

However, reincarnation does solve some of man's basic questions and concerns. If a person sees good deeds as the means to heaven, he can become frustrated with his lack of progress toward perfection. But in reincarnation, man has many lives to better himself. This system allows an individual to solve the problem of his sin on his own.

Reincarnation can be appealing to a society raised on the notion that you get only what you pay for. And it explains the pain and suffering of the apparently innocent. People suffer because of the sins in their past lives, so God is not to blame. By requiring a man to stay on the treadmill of rebirth until he is sinless, reincarnation overcomes the problem of asking God to approve evil.

Granting that reincarnation solves some problems, when we look at it closely, it creates more problems than it solves.

First, since new souls are not created, life should be improving as man progresses through the purification process. The problem is that we see just as much, if not more, evil in the world today as there was 100 years ago.

Second, why is the population of the world increasing and not decreasing as the theory would lead us to think? The traditional reincarnationist answers this objection by saying that souls have been transmigrating not only in humans, but also in other living forms. It should follow that as the human population increases, the population of other life forms should decrease. But a study of nature does not reveal this to be true.

Third, if we were all to espouse reincarnation, our world would be virtually devoid of compassion and care for those who suffer. Remember, suffering comes as a result of sins in previous lives. Since karma never allows for the forgiveness of sin, but demands that payment always be made, we are actually robbing people of the opportunity to atone for their sins in this life if we ease their suffering now. The concept of karma allows no room for grace.

Fourth, how do lower forms of life like worms and mollusks build good karma? Will a roach be incarnated into a higher form if it stays out of people's kitchens? Morality requires the ability to make a conscious choice, and this is quite different from blind obedience to instinct.

The most difficult problem for reincarnation is that it contradicts Scripture. In this chapter, we examined a number of passages that teach the impossibility of salvation through man's efforts. A review of these verses would be helpful. In addition, Christ repudiated the law of karma in John 9:1-3. If karma prevailed, the blind man's condition would have resulted from his own sin. But Christ said, "It was neither that this man sinned, nor his parents" (John 9:3). Also, 2 Corinthians 5:21 says that Christ substituted Himself for us so that we could be made righteous through Him.

This concept of forgiveness of sin is foreign to reincarnation. Karma demands payment and requires suffering, while Christ pays the penalty and offers forgiveness. What a contrast!

Hebrews 9:27 tells us, "It is appointed for men to die *once,* and after this comes judgment." This, as we learn in John 3:18, comes as a result of rejecting Christ and His payment. John 5:24 explains that by receiving Christ, one is removed from this judgment.

The famous Indian leader Gandhi expressed the frustration that millions face when they attempt to achieve perfection through their works. Near the end of a life of tirelessly giving himself for others, he confessed in his autobiography, *The Story of My Experiments with Truth:*

> To attain to perfect purity one has to become absolutely passion-free in thought, speech and action . . . I know that I have not in me as yet that triple purity, in spite of constant ceaseless striving for it. That is why the world's praise fails to move me; indeed it very often stings me. To conquer the subtle passions seems to me harder far than the physical conquest of the world by the force of arms (pp. 504-05).

If Gandhi could not achieve it with the sacrificial life he led, who can? A system of works always brings frustration and failure, whereas Christ offers forgiveness and freedom. The choice is ours.

12

Isn't Salvation By Faith Too Simple?

Often-Asked Questions:

Isn't just believing too easy?
You don't get something for nothing. Why should it be any different with salvation?
Doesn't the Bible say, "God helps those who help themselves?"
What happens to the incentive for being good?
Why would anyone appreciate salvation if it were free?

Two Options

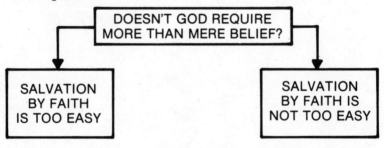

(CHART 58)

When people hear that all a person has to do to obtain the gift of salvation is receive Jesus Christ and His payment for sin, some balk at the idea. They argue that this is too easy; just believing is not enough. Salvation must be earned if it is to be appreciated. But the Scriptures affirm that while salvation is free, it is not easy. (See Chart 58.)

First Option: Salvation by Faith Is Too Easy

There are many who shudder at the concept of salvation being a gift. Salvation must be earned, they think, for everyone knows you never get something for nothing. If your friends stress that salvation must be earned, then you must first deal with the question of good works (see chapter 11).

Behind this position is the notion that nothing of value is ever truly free. But something could be of value and free to us if it was paid for by someone else. When a son gets a new car as a graduation gift, it is free to him. But his parents had to pay the price.

Another argument for this position says that if salvation is ours for the taking, it would remove all incentive for righteous living. Why not receive Christ and then go out and live any way we want, indulging any whim? Paul addresses this very issue in Romans 6:1-2. He has just developed the theme that salvation is by grace, not by works. Realizing that some may question a man's motives once he is guaranteed salvation, Paul queries, "What shall we say then? Are we to continue in sin that grace might increase?" His response: "May it never be! How shall we who died to sin still live in it?" When a person understands the greatness of God's salvation and the riches of His mercy, he will not seek ways to violate his relationship with God. Rather, he will want to cultivate his relationship with God.

The big problem with the idea that salvation by faith is too easy is that it contradicts the biblical record. Ephesians 2:8-9 clearly states, "For by grace you have been saved through faith; and that not of yourselves, it is the gift of God; not as a result of works, that no one should boast." For a more detailed scriptural refutation of this untenable view, review chapter 11.

Chart 59 depicts the first option.

Second Option: Salvation by Faith Is Not Too Easy

The gift of salvation had to be free, because man's problem of achieving salvation is not difficult—it's impossible. Christ made this clear in Matthew 5:48: "Therefore you are to be perfect, as your heavenly Father is perfect." Paul tells us that "all have sinned and fall

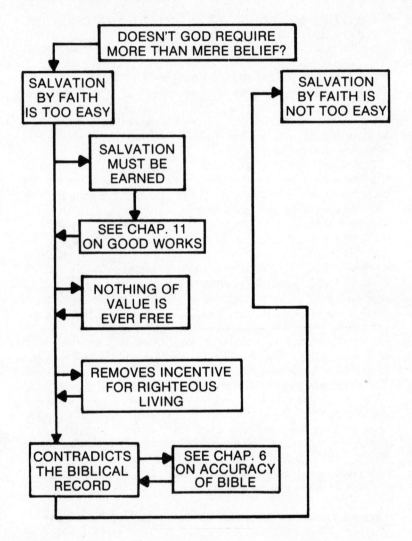

(CHART 59)

short of the glory of God" (Rom. 3:23).

Free is not the same as easy, however. The plan of salvation was not easy for the Father. He had to separate Himself from His Son (Matt. 27:46). The plan of salvation was not easy for the Son. He humbled Himself (Phil. 2:5-8), paid the penalty for our sins (2 Cor. 5:21), and was separated from the Father. And the plan of salvation is not easy for man. He has to give up his pride and admit there is nothing he can do to make himself worthy before the Father (Titus 3:5).

Imagine a wealthy man knocking on your door. When you open it he says, "I understand your dream car is a $120,000 slate gray Rolls Royce. How would you like to have one?"

Your eyes glaze over, and then you come to your senses and tell him, "I don't know how to put together a magnificent machine like that. I don't know the difference between a drive shaft and a camshaft. Besides, I haven't got near enough money to purchase such a car."

The gentleman responds, "You don't understand. The car has already been put together by expert craftsmen, and it's here in your driveway. I have paid for it myself. Here are the keys. All you must do is accept them."

The fact that the automobile is being offered free of charge does not make it easy to assemble or purchase.

Electricity also illustrates something that appears easy but really isn't. Most of us take electricity for granted when we use it in our homes. We have only to flick a switch, and electricity produces light, sound, or a picture on the television. Electrical current boils water, dries our hair, washes the dishes, and keeps us cool.

But it wasn't easy for the electricians who wired our homes. Nor is it easy for the utilities to produce electricity or restore power when the lines have been broken due to a storm.

It would be foolish for someone to reject something of value just because it is free. Imagine that your ship has sunk in the middle of the ocean. Days go by as you bob up and down in your life jacket. You know it is impossible to swim to shore, and it looks as if there is no hope. Suddenly, a ship appears on the horizon and eventually pulls alongside you. Some of the crew throw you a life preserver and it lands just an arm's reach away. Would you ask the ship to back off a mile so that you could feel you had earned your rescue? The answer is obvious.

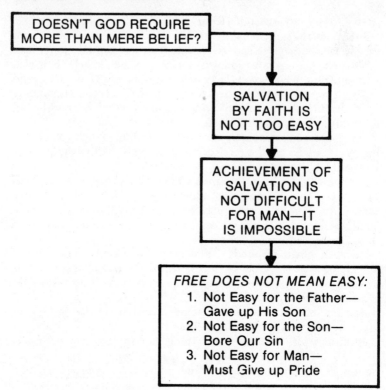

(CHART 60)

So it is with Christ. As man bobs through the sea of life, he is hopelessly lost with no chance of survival. Christ comes alongside us and offers salvation. Should His offer be rejected just because it is free?

Chart 60 shows the second option.

Summary and Flow Chart

Confusion arises when salvation is presented as a gift. Many feel this is too easy, and man should earn his way to God. But this runs contrary to Scripture. Salvation is free because we are incapable of

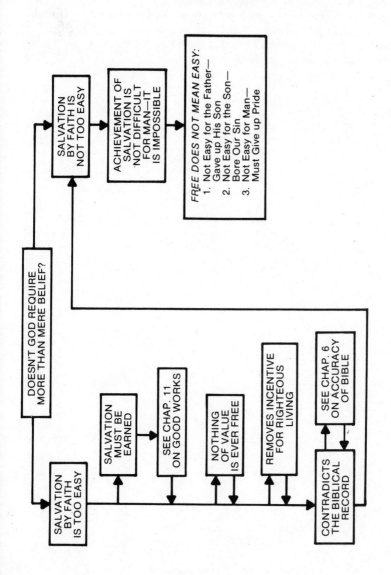

(CHART 61)

earning it. God's standard is perfection, and Christ makes it available to us through His perfect life and sacrifice. Though the offer of salvation is free, it wasn't easy for the Father or the Son, and it is not easy for man in his pride to accept.

13

What Does The Bible Mean By *Believe?*

Often-Asked Questions:

How much faith do you have to have?
Doesn't everyone believe in Christ and His existence?
What if I want to believe but still have doubts?
Don't you have to stop sinning to believe in Christ?

Two Options

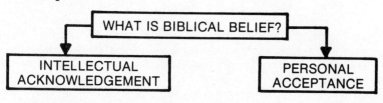

(CHART 62)

There are more than 14,000 meanings for the 500 most commonly used words. With so many meanings for so few words, there is a lot of opportunity for miscommunication. It is therefore important when we seek to communicate with others that all parties involved are on the same wavelength. If this is true in everyday conversation, how much more essential is it to define our terms properly when eternity is at stake in what we discuss?

The first option for the word *believe* defines it as an intellectual acknowledgment of a set of facts. The second option calls not only for an intellectual acknowledgment but also for a personal acceptance of the truth.

First Option: Intellectual Acknowledgment

If we followed common usage, the sentence *"I believe in tornadoes"* would mean that we give intellectual acknowledgment to the existence of tornadoes. If we say we believe in George Washington or Susan B. Anthony, we are giving intellectual acknowledgment that they existed. This is a belief about someone or something. But James tells us that a belief that encompasses only intellectual assent is not enough. The demons have this type of belief (James 2:19). They recognize the existence of Christ and all the works He performed, but this belief does not save them.

The New Testament usage of the term *believe* carries the concept further than the popular usage of the term. John 1:12 says, "But as many as *received* Him, to them He gave the right to become children of God, even to those who believe in His name." So a biblical belief not only involves intellectual assent but also personal acceptance. It is not just believing *about* Christ; it is believing *in* Christ, or more accurately, believing into Christ. This denotes a belief or faith that takes man out of himself and puts him into Christ. Biblical belief, then, is more than an acknowledgment of Christ's existence and death. It requires a trusting of one's self to Jesus. A person believes in Christ if he personally receives Christ's payment for his sin. This means a change in attitude so that he no longer relies on his own efforts to obtain salvation but trusts in Jesus Christ alone as his only hope of reconciliation with God.

Where is the crossover from one type of belief to the other? Perhaps the following illustration will help. Once a country boy ventured into the big city of Knoxville, Tennessee. He wanted to visit a friend in Memphis and decided to go by plane. He had never flown before, and this was his first trip to an airport. When he arrived, he looked over the departures and arrivals board and noticed that the plane for Memphis left Knoxville at 10:30 A.M. and arrived at its destination at 10:30 A.M. Not realizing the time zone change between the two cities, he was really puzzled by the departure and arrival times, so he asked the ticket agent if the times were correct. "Oh yes," she said. "Would you like to purchase a ticket?" He said, "No, not yet," and went to a window to observe the planes. A little while later he noticed a different agent at the counter, so he went and asked again. The second person concurred that the times were correct and asked if he wanted to buy a ticket. His quick reply was, "No, ma'am, I'd just like to be around when that thing takes off!"

He believed what was said *about* the plane was true. He had an intellectual acknowledgment that the plane would do what the departure board said it would. But he was unwilling to believe *in* the plane and purchase a ticket for himself.

During the Middle Ages, three words were used to describe the different levels of belief: (1) *noticia* (notice)—observe the facts objectively; (2) *assentia* (assent)—acknowledge this truth intellectually; and (3) *fiducia* (faith)—receive the solution personally. Let's apply these words to the Gospel message. On the first level, we notice the facts to be believed. We are sinners, and the penalty for our sin is death and separation from God. On the cross, Christ paid the penalty for our sins and made the gift of eternal life available to us. On the second level, we not only notice the facts but also acknowledge their truth intellectually. Up to this point we still just believe *about* Christ. For us to believe *in* Christ, we need to move on to our third concept, *fiducia*. We must now place our trust in Christ alone for the forgiveness of our personal sins. When we go to level three, we have received the free gift of salvation from Christ, but not before. Salvation comes not from an intellectual acknowledgment but from a belief that personally receives Christ's offer.

Before we examine our second option, Chart 63 shows the first option.

Second Option: Personal Acceptance

As we saw in our examination of John 1:12, *believe* equals *receive*. The concept of receiving Christ is consistent with several other passages in Scripture.

"Now I make known to you, brethren, the Gospel which I preached to you, which also you *received,* in which also you stand" (1 Cor. 15:1). "For I delivered to you as of first importance what I also *received,* that Christ died for our sins according to the Scriptures" (1 Cor. 15:3). "As you therefore have *received* Christ Jesus the Lord, so walk in Him" (Col. 2:6). "And with all the deception of wickedness for those who perish, because they did not *receive* the love of the truth

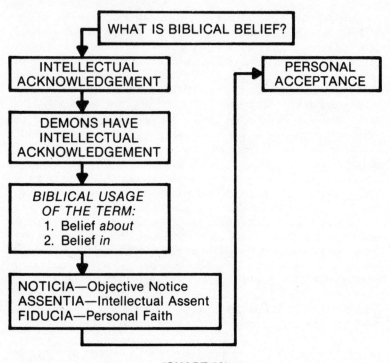

(CHART 63)

so as to be saved" (2 Thes. 2:10). The notion that biblical belief equals receiving Christ is further substantiated by the way salvation is described as a *gift* in several passages (Rom. 5:17; 6:23; Eph. 2:8-9).

Inherent in the idea of a gift is that it must be received from the giver, and this is true of the gift of salvation. Biblically, believing and receiving are synonymous, and John 1:12 uses both terms with the clear intent of equating the two actions. Imagine parents who want to give a gift to their young son. As they hold it in their hands, their son gazes at it, overwhelmed by his parents' love, and profusely thanks them for the gift. Yet the gift remains in the parents' hands. What's the problem? The son has done everything but receive the gift by reaching out and appropriating it from his parents. So it is with the gift of salvation—God extends His gift, and every individual must personally receive it from Him.

A person can doubt Christ and His credentials or he can believe that Christ was who He said He was. But until he claims Christ's offer for himself, he is no better off than the person who doesn't believe at all.

A man and a woman came before a clergyman to be married. The clergyman asked the bride, "Will you take this man to be your lawfully wedded husband?"

"Oh," she answered, "he's really handsome, isn't he?"

So the clergyman tried again, "Will you take this man as your husband?"

"Oh, I think he's so nice," she replied, and then added, "I think he'll be a wonderful husband and provider."

It's obvious here that the bride needs to say "I do." When she has said "I do," the groom will become her husband, but not before. She must accept him, just as each person must go beyond mere acknowledgment of Jesus Christ. Each individual must receive Christ not just as the Saviour of the world but as his personal Saviour.

Picture a man who falls from a cliff. As he plunges down, he reaches out and grabs a small limb. He hangs on, looks up, and sees the sheer precipice above. He looks down and sees jagged peaks reaching up for his straining body, and begins to despair. Suddenly, he sees an angel above him and begins to scream, "Save me!"

"Do you believe I *can* save you?" the angel asks.

The man sees the strong wings, the mighty arms. He says, "Yes, I believe you can save me."

"Do you believe I *will* save you?"

The man sees the compassionate, merciful face. "Yes, yes, I believe!" he cries.

"Then," says the angel, "LET GO!"

Still clinging, the man yells, "Is there anybody else up there?"

You see, you may believe that Jesus *can* save you. That's essential, but it is not enough. You may be confident that He *will* save you. That's also necessary, but it is not real belief. To trust in Jesus Christ is to let go of every other confidence, of every other trust, and of every other security, and to cast yourself on Him as your only hope of salvation.

Charles Blondin, a Frenchman, was one of the world's finest tightrope walkers. In 1860 he successfully crossed the treacherous Niagara Falls (approximately a 1,000-foot span, 160 feet above the raging waters) on a tightrope. He then turned to the gathered crowd that was awestruck by this incredible feat and asked how many believed he could traverse the tightrope a second time pushing a wheelbarrow. The enthusiastic crowd cheered, acknowledging their belief in Blondin. Blondin succeeded, and then addressed the astonished crowd again, "Does anyone believe enough in me to get in the wheelbarrow and cross Niagara Falls with me?" No one volunteered! Finally, Blondin's manager climbed on Blondin's back, and they crossed the great chasm together. Christ said that there is a great chasm between man and God, and the only way to get from one side to the other is through Him.

Sometimes it helps to use a frivolous illustration to get the point across. For example, there is the story about a man who was afflicted with an acute pain in his right side. The doctor's diagnosis was appendicitis, and he felt it was absolutely necessary for the patient to have an emergency appendectomy. The patient was skeptical of the doctor's abilities, so he asked the doctor if he had any proof to support his diagnosis. It just so happened that the doctor was having a reunion of all his past appendectomy patients.

The nurse wheeled the sick man down the corridor in front of the doctor's previous patients, and all of them enthusiastically testified that the doctor had successfully cured them of the same kind of pain by performing appendectomies.

"OK," the man said, "I believe, Doctor, that you are capable of removing my appendix and eliminating the pain."

"Fine," the doctor replied. "Now please sign this consent form right here."

"Oh, no," the man responded, "you're not going to cut me open!"

The patient's belief was not true belief if he didn't allow the doctor to operate. We can believe that Christ diagnosed our problem correctly, and we can even believe that He has a 100 percent cure rate, but if we don't allow Him to operate on us personally, our belief is not a saving one.

When we tell others about Christ, it is important that we clearly communicate the biblical concept of belief. One of the easiest ways Satan can keep people from trusting Christ is to have God's servants

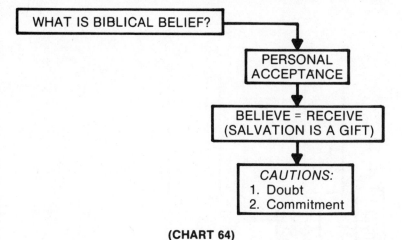

WHAT IS BIBLICAL BELIEF?

PERSONAL ACCEPTANCE

BELIEVE = RECEIVE (SALVATION IS A GIFT)

CAUTIONS:
1. Doubt
2. Commitment

(CHART 64)

distort this concept. We should watch two things very carefully here:

The first is *doubt.* Some feel they can't decide for Christ until all their doubts are removed. It is imperative that we dispel this roadblock to Christ. Faith is not the absence of doubt, it is a decision based on the evidence at hand. A person can have some doubts about doing something and still make the decision to do it. Suppose two men have equal doubts about the safety of flying. A special opportunity arises for both men, but it means they must fly. Both continue to have their doubts, but one man decides to get on the plane while the other stays behind. So it is with Christianity; doubt doesn't have to inhibit a person from receiving Christ. It is a matter of choice, a step taken in spite of doubts.

The second thing we need to watch is *commitment.* Some people have labored over receiving Christ as their Saviour because they felt that a promise to subject every area of their lives to the control of God forever had to go hand in hand with the decision. It is true that biblical belief requires commitment, but this is not so much a commitment to what we are going to do in the future as it is a commitment to what Jesus Christ has done in the past. In many cases, an understanding of total commitment to the lordship of Christ is not achieved until some time after salvation. It is an unfortunate reality

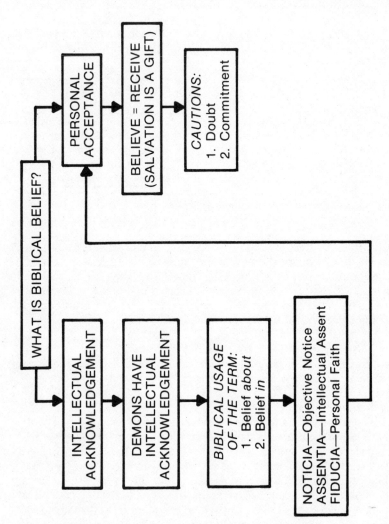

(CHART 65)

that many Christians acknowledge that Jesus is Lord and Master but still try to run their own lives.

To "believe in Christ" is to understand who Jesus Christ is and what He did for you, to agree with God that you need Him alone as your substitute for your sin, and to invite Him to personally enter your life (John 5:24).

Chart 64 shows option two.

Summary and Flow Chart

We first considered the idea that biblical belief means an intellectual acknowledgment of the facts of Christ and His work. But demons have that much belief, so we delved into Scripture for further insight into the term *believe.* The biblical term means more than mere belief *about* something; it means belief *in* something or someone. It is an intellectual acknowledgment that leads to a personal reception of Christ and His offer of salvation.

Second, we defended the idea that *believe* equals *receive,* and we looked at corollary passages to John 1:12. Salvation is depicted in Scripture as a gift, and we are called to receive that gift. We offered a few illustrations to help clarify the definition of *believe,* and stressed two cautions at the end: First, faith is not the absence of doubt. You can have doubts and still receive Christ. Second, the commitment made in accepting Christ is not a commitment to what we are going to do in the future. It is a commitment to what He has done for us in the past.

14

Can Anyone Be Sure
of His Salvation?

Often-Asked Questions:

Can't a Christian simply stop believing in Christ?

Aren't there certain sins that could cause a person to lose his salvation?

Will God let someone into heaven who claims to believe in Jesus but lives an immoral life?

Salvation is appropriated by faith, but doesn't a person need to maintain it?

Don't some verses teach that a Christian can "fall from grace"?

Two Options

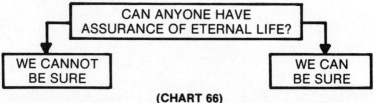

(CHART 66)

If getting into heaven depended on our good works as well as our faith in Christ, none of us could say with any confidence that we *know* we are going to heaven. This is the first option. We could never be sure if we were working enough or sinning too much. No Christian could rest in the finished work of Christ, because, somehow, it would not be sufficient. Christian service would be prompted at least partly out of a desire to maintain that which otherwise could be lost. In contrast, the other option affirms that the believer *can* be assured of eternal life, because it is based solely upon the redemptive work of Christ, not our performance. (See Chart 66.)

First Option: We Cannot Be Sure of Eternal Life

When people gain some understanding of what it means to believe in Christ (chapter 13), they will sometimes raise the question of assurance. In most cases, this question is not so much an objection to Christianity as it is a request for clarification of the Gospel.

The real issue is what God's Word says about the matter of assurance, and not how we feel about it. An explanation of the meaning of God's gift of eternal life, along with a few biblical passages, may be all that is necessary to answer this question. But sometimes people will have specific objections to the idea of assurance, and when this happens, these objections will have to be met.

One of these objections has to do with the nature of *faith*. Can't someone stop believing in Christ, and wouldn't this cause him to lose his salvation? All of us have heard of people who said, "I tried Christianity once, but it just didn't work." But was it really Christianity that they tried? For others, the church was a prominent part of their lives as they were growing up. They appeared to be zealous Christians, but after their first year in college, they wrote Christianity off as another religious delusion. In cases like these, it may be that they were never reborn. They did not lose their salvation if they did not have it to begin with.

As we discussed under the question about the hypocrites (chapter 10), there is a problem of confusing *profession* of salvation with *possession* of salvation. "Not everyone who says to Me, 'Lord, Lord,' will enter the kingdom of heaven" (Matt. 7:21; see 7:22-23). Many people claim to be Christians who have not really come to grips with the Gospel. Others claim that they lost their faith, but theirs may not have been a saving faith in the first place.

This does not mean that a genuine Christian will not stop believing. There are times when many true believers experience profound doubts due to circumstances or intellectual problems. It can be healthy to wrestle with honest doubts about the faith, because this process can strengthen one's understanding. The Christian who never consciously wonders, "Is all of this really true? How do I know I'm not deluding myself?" will probably not have as firm a grasp of the basis for his faith as the one who struggles through these questions.

When doubts arise, they do not put a Christian's salvation in jeopardy. A visitor in Manhattan may decide to take the elevator up to the observation floor of the World Trade Center. When he steps on and the elevator begins to move, he has made an irrevocable decision that commits him to the whole quarter-mile vertical journey. He may be gripped with a sudden panic after 30 seconds and 55 floors, fully convinced that the cable will break. But this does not change the fact that he will safely arrive at the 107th floor. Similarly, coming to Christ does not involve intellectual assent alone but a willful choice to place one's eternal destiny in the hands of the Saviour. This choice needs to be made only once; then regardless of how we feel, He will bring us safely to our destination.

Another objection relates to the nature of *sin*. Can't a Christian be disqualified by the practice of certain sins? The problem here is that many people make an artificial distinction between "big" and "little" sins that reflects human law codes more than God's attitude. In our system, murder and armed robbery are far more serious offenses than lying and cheating, while greed and arrogance count as nothing. But God regards the *intent* to murder or commit adultery as seriously as the acts themselves: "You have heard that it was said, 'You shall not commit adultery'; but I say to you, that everyone who looks on a woman to lust for her has committed adultery with her already in his heart" (Matt. 5:27-28). John wrote in his first epistle, "Everyone who hates his brother is a murderer" (1 John 3:15). In God's sight, sins like jealousy, anger, malice, slander, pride, bitterness, and envy are not minor offenses. Thus, if any sins can disqualify someone as a Christian, all of us would be disqualified.

An alternate way of approaching this objection is to ask, "What is good enough to get you into heaven, and what is bad enough to keep you out of heaven?" God does not hold some kind of scale that weighs our good works against our bad. If this were the case, a "score" of 51 percent good would make it, so that people who are up to 49 percent evil would be allowed into His presence. The whole idea is ludicrous—even an Ivory Soap percentage (99 and 44/100 percent) would not be good enough. In His Sermon on the Mount, Jesus said, "Therefore you are to be perfect, as your heavenly Father is perfect"

(Matt. 5:48). God will accept nothing less than perfection. As we saw in chapter 11, He does not grade on a curve. Our only hope of salvation, then, is the perfect righteousness of Jesus Christ which is imparted to those who trust in Him. If perfection is required for salvation, anything less than that would disqualify us. This means that even if a Christian's salvation were only one percent dependent upon the avoidance of sin, he would stand condemned because he could not fulfill that one percent. Any sin of commission or omission would cause him to fall short.

Yet another objection relates to the nature of *works*. Doesn't a Christian have to *maintain* his relationship to God and thus his salvation? No, because salvation is a gift by God's grace; it must be by grace since no one deserves it. It is maintained by His power, not by our performance. Jude's doxology is addressed "to Him who is able to keep you from stumbling, and to make you stand in the presence of His glory blameless with great joy" (Jude 24). *He* is the one who keeps us from stumbling, because we could not otherwise keep ourselves blameless. Titus 3:4-7 is one of the clearest biblical portraits of God's grace on our behalf:

> But when the kindness of God our Saviour and His love for mankind appeared, He saved us, not on the basis of deeds which we have done in righteousness, but according to His mercy, by the washing of regeneration and renewing by the Holy Spirit, whom He poured out upon us richly through Jesus Christ our Saviour, that being justified by His grace we might be made heirs according to the hope of eternal life.

Christ's righteousness has been imputed to us—placed, as it were, on our account. This is *His* righteousness, and by His grace it has become ours; it is not jeopardized by our behavior. Speaking of the Father and the Son, Paul stated, "He made Him who knew no sin to be sin on our behalf, that we might become the righteousness of God in Him" (2 Cor. 5:21). It is evident from passages like these that not only salvation but also sanctification is achieved by faith. Any good works that follow should be a product of this living faith, accomplished by the Spirit. Indeed, belief should lead to behavior, and if we do not see any qualitative changes in a person's life, we might wonder whether that person's faith is real (see James 2:14-26). There is a danger, however, of falling into the mind-set that salvation is achieved by the principle of grace and maintained by the principle of works. Along similar lines, Paul denounced the Galatians when he wrote, "Are you so foolish? Having begun by the Spirit, are you now being perfected by the flesh?" (Gal. 3:3)

When Christ paid for our sins almost 2,000 years ago, He knew us though we did not yet exist. At that point, all our sins were future events, but He knew them all and paid for them all. It is theological nonsense to say that He paid only for those sins which we would commit prior to believing in Him but not for those sins which we would commit after believing in Him. Either He paid for them all or He paid for none; a partial redemption is no redemption in God's sight.

If someone decided to pay off the mortgage on your house, you would be notified to that effect, and your monthly house payment would be returned if it reached the bank after the note had been paid. It would be absurd for the bank to take your check and send you a letter stating that even though the mortgage had been paid off, you must still pay it because it was your mortgage. When a debt has been paid in full, it no longer exists.

Christ not only *saves* us but also *sustains* us. When a father holds the hand of his little girl as they walk together, he guides her and keeps her from the danger of the street. Because she is not yet proficient at walking, she may begin to trip several times, but his grip is sufficient to keep her from falling. What father would hold a child's hand while she is safe but let loose the moment she began to fall? In the same way, our hands are firmly held by Him who loved us to the end. Salvation is based on God's ability, not ours.

Many people definitely have trusted in Jesus Christ but have no assurance of eternal life. In the case of genuine believers, there are two contributing causes for this. One is that a number of Christians are unaware of the biblical teaching on assurance. As a result, they fall into one or more of the three misunderstandings we just discussed (a problem concerning the nature of faith, the nature of sin, or the nature of works).

The first contributing cause relates to the mind, but the second relates to the emotions. Even if a believer *understands* the truth about assurance, he may not *feel* secure in Christ. While emotions are important, they do not determine or measure our position before God. Doubts and depressed feelings do not change what God says is true. It is imperative that we reason from the truth of God's Word rather than our feelings. Our responsibility is to choose by faith to believe what God says; and when we honor God in this way, we create an environment in which His Spirit can gradually conform our feelings to the truth. Reasoning from man (our practice) to God will lead to insecurity and fear, but reasoning from God (our position) to man will lead to confidence and peace.

The first option on the issue of assurance is shown in Chart 67.

Second Option: We Can Be Sure of Eternal Life

The nature of a gift and of eternal life. Eternal life must be a gift, because we could never hope to earn it. When a person grasps the meaning of a gift and of eternal life, together with some key biblical passages on assurance, he will begin to understand that those who trust in Christ can *know* that they have eternal life.

Because salvation is a gift (John 3:16; Rom. 5:15-16; 2 Cor. 9:15), it cannot be earned, but must be accepted with empty hands. God paid our debt in full, and we have been set free from our bondage. Nothing more remains to be paid.

If a friend gave you a book as a birthday present, you would not offer to pay him back—only a word of gratitude would be appropriate. An attempt to pay for a present would defeat the whole concept of a gift, and could even insult the giver. If you pay for something, it can no longer be regarded as a gift.

In addition, when a gift is received, the recipient should not have to work to keep it. If a father gave his son some camping equipment as a gift and later took it away because he did not clean his room, it was not a gift after all. Instead, it was a wage that was conditioned on the fulfillment of certain tasks. God's gift of salvation is different, because the sole condition is that a person must reach out and take it by an act of faith (chapter 13). Because it is a gift, it is not maintained by our works. Nor is it the kind of gift that can be given back. The gift of forgiveness and acceptance cannot be received and then returned. When Christ's righteousness is placed on our account, it is there to stay.

People frequently object to this concept of an unconditional gift: "If a Christian doesn't have to maintain his salvation, why can't he go off and sin as much as he wants?" Another variation is the hypothetical "what if?" scenario—"What if a person believes in

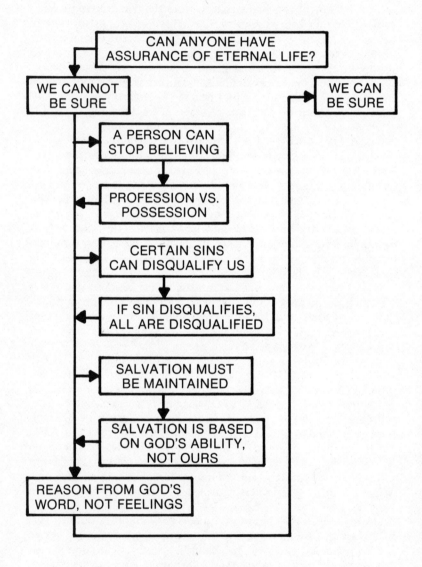

(CHART 67)

Christ and then commits 20 murders? Are you going to tell me that God would still let him into heaven?" Sometimes people really want to press their point by using the worst example they can think of: "Do you mean that if Adolph Hitler had repented and received Christ, God would have let him off the hook for his atrocities?"

To answer this kind of objection, stress that it is never wise to build a doctrine on hypothetical situations. It is theoretically possible that the roof may cave in on your house next week, but that is no basis for moving your family out. We need to build on reality, not idle speculation. How many people do you know who have trusted in Christ and then committed 20 murders? It is helpful to look at the *real* effect that knowing Jesus has on people's lives. When a person makes a genuine commitment to Christ, things gradually begin to change. Paul wrote that "if any man is in Christ, he is a new creature; the old things passed away; behold; new things have come" (2 Cor. 5:17). New interests and desires begin to surface, and the believer finds that he can no longer indulge in old sinful patterns without conviction by the Spirit. When he does get enmeshed in sin, he will be disciplined by his heavenly Father, who loves him too much to allow him to stray very far without consequences. "For those whom the Lord loves He disciplines, and He scourges every son whom He receives" (Heb. 12:6).

When a person becomes a Christian, he acknowledges his sin and turns to Christ for forgiveness. He does not say, "Well, now that I've got my fire and life insurance, I can sin with impunity." Paul wrote that "where sin increased, grace abounded all the more" (Rom. 5:20), but was quick to add that no Christian should ever abuse the grace of God: "What shall we say then? Are we to continue in sin that grace might increase? May it never be! How shall we who died to sin still live in it?" (Rom. 6:1-2) Paul added that "our old self was crucified with Him, that our body of sin might be done away with, that we should no longer be slaves to sin" (Rom. 6:6).

Sin is incompatible with the believer's new self, and he does not have to succumb to it. But when he does, he will find that sin still has its consequences. As a person matures in Christ, he discovers that what he previously may have imagined to be a dreary life turns out to be the greatest adventure of all. A life of abiding in Christ is so much more abundant (John 10:10) than a life of putting self first.

Thus, when someone becomes a Christian, there *should* be some changes in his life. If, after a number of months, there are no qualitative changes in his actions or attitudes, he may just be professing but not possessing a relationship with Jesus Christ.

We saw that a gift cannot be purchased or earned or conditionally maintained. If any of these things were necessary, it would no longer be free. The meaning of eternal life is also important to the issue of assurance of salvation. Eternal life cannot be lost, because it is unlimited. If a person could somehow lose it, what he had was limited life, not eternal life. Christ says that eternal life is the present possession of each believer: "Truly, truly, I say to you, he who hears My word, and believes Him who sent Me, has eternal life, and does not come into judgment, but has passed out of death into life" (John 5:24).

But eternal life is even more than endless existence or a new quality of life; it is the very life of Christ in the believer. Only God is eternal (no beginning and no end), and He implants the eternal life of Christ into a person the moment he is born into the family of God. This new life is ours by a new birth (John 3:3-8; 1 Peter 1:3, 23), and though we may disobey our heavenly Father, we are still His children. If most imperfect earthly fathers will never abandon their children, how much more will the child of God be accepted by his perfect heavenly Father? We may hinder our *fellowship* with God, but our *relationship* as His children is secure.

Without the assurance of this irrevocable relationship, there would be no joy or rest in the Christian life. If God accepted us on the basis of performance, we would all live in constant fear and insecurity. Our Christian service would be motivated by a desire to earn merit with God, and grace would no longer be grace. It is impossible to merit unmerited favor (grace).

Some object that it is arrogant on our part to say that we know we will get into heaven. At first blush this may seem to be arrogant, but a closer look reveals just the opposite. It is the person who has the delusion that he can earn his way to heaven who is being arrogant, not the one who acknowledges that his salvation comes solely by the grace of God.

Biblical passages on assurance. Numerous biblical verses affirm the security of the child of God. Here are 12, listed in New Testament order:

(1) *John 3:16:* "For God so loved the world, that He gave His

only begotten Son, that whoever believes in Him should not perish, but have eternal life." The only condition for eternal life is faith in Christ.

(2) *John 5:24:* "Truly, truly, I say to you, he who hears My word, and believes Him who sent Me, has eternal life, and does not come into judgment, but has passed out of death into life." Jesus promises three things to those who believe in Him: (a) the *present possession* of eternal life, (b) exemption from a judgment of condemnation, and (c) a new position of spiritual life before God. A contract is no better than the people behind it—if we can believe men, why not Christ? Having believed in Him, the fulfillment of His promises depends on Him, not us.

(3) *John 6:37, 44:* "All that the Father gives Me shall come to Me, and the one who comes to Me I will certainly not cast out. . . . No one can come to Me, unless the Father who sent Me draws him; and I will raise him up on the last day." Everyone who comes to Christ has been drawn by the Father and given to the Son.

(4) *John 10:28-29:* "And I give eternal life to them, and they shall never perish; and no one shall snatch them out of My hand. My Father, who has given them to Me, is greater than all; and no one is able to snatch them out of the Father's hand." Christ's sheep are held securely in His hands and in the Father's hands. No force, including ourselves, can remove us from His grasp.

(5) *Romans 8:1, 16:* "There is therefore now no condemnation for those who are in Christ Jesus. . . . The Spirit Himself bears witness with our spirit that we are children of God." The believer should have no fear of condemnation but a spirit of adoption as one who knows he is a child of God.

(6) *Romans 8:29-35, 38-39:* "For whom He foreknew, He also predestined to become conformed to the image of His Son, that He might be the first-born among many brethren; and whom He predestined, these He also called; and whom He called, these He also justified; and whom He justified, these He also glorified. What then shall we say to these things? If God is for us, who is against us? He who did not spare His own Son, but delivered Him up for us all, how will He not also with Him freely give us all things? Who will bring a charge against God's elect? God is the one who justifies; who is the one who condemns? Christ Jesus is He who died, yes, rather who was raised, who is at the right hand of God, who also intercedes for us.

Who shall separate us from the love of Christ? Shall tribulation, or distress, or persecution, or famine, or nakedness, or peril, or sword? . . . For I am convinced that neither death, nor life, nor angels, nor principalities, nor things present, nor things to come, nor powers, nor height, nor depth, nor any other created thing, shall be able to separate us from the love of God, which is in Christ Jesus our Lord." This magnificent passage tells us that once a person is in Christ, nothing at all (including himself) can separate him from Christ. This relationship becomes timeless and irrevocable.

(7) *Ephesians 1:4:* "Just as He chose us in Him before the foundation of the world, that we should be holy and blameless before Him." God knew us even before the creation of the cosmos and planned that believers would become perfectly conformed to the image of His Son.

(8) *Ephesians 1:13-14:* "In Him, you also, after listening to the message of truth, the Gospel of your salvation—having also believed, you were sealed in Him with the Holy Spirit of promise, who is given as a pledge of our inheritance, with a view to the redemption of God's own possession, to the praise of His glory." Every Christian is sealed with the Holy Spirit, and this divine seal will not be removed until we obtain our heavenly inheritance.

(9) *Colossians 1:12-14:* "Giving thanks to the Father, who has qualified us to share in the inheritance of the saints in light. For He delivered us from the domain of darkness, and transferred us to the kingdom of His beloved Son, in whom we have redemption, the forgiveness of sins." Believers have already been placed in Christ's kingdom; His redemptive work has already been accomplished.

(10) *1 Peter 1:3-4:* "Blessed be the God and Father of our Lord Jesus Christ, who according to His great mercy has caused us to be born again to a living hope through the resurrection of Jesus Christ from the dead, to obtain an inheritance which is imperishable and undefiled and will not fade away, reserved in heaven for you." As believers, our incorruptible inheritance is reserved for us by God.

(11) *1 John 2:1:* "My little children, I am writing these things to you that you may not sin. And if anyone sins, we have an Advocate with the Father, Jesus Christ the righteous; and He Himself is the propitiation for our sins; and not for ours only, but also for those of the whole world." When believers sin, Christ stands as our Advocate and satisfies the Father because of His once-for-all sacrifice.

(12) *1 John 5:13:* "These things I have written to you who believe in the name of the Son of God, in order that you may know that you have eternal life." Believers can *know* for sure.

The Greek word translated "believe" (*pisteuo*) is used in the aorist tense in key passages about salvation. This tense refers to something that is made complete at a point in time rather than progressive action (see John 1:12; Acts 16:31; Rom. 4:3). The New Testament repeatedly emphasizes that faith in Christ is the only condition for salvation. Here are just some of the verses that teach this: Luke 7:48-50; 8:12; John 1:12; 3:15-16, 36; 6:29, 35, 40, 47; 7:38-39; 8:24; 9:35-38; 11:26; 12:36, 46; 14:1; 17:21; 19:35; 20:29, 31; Acts 3:16; 8:12; 10:43; 11:17, 21; 13:39; 14:27; 15:7, 9; 16:31; 18:27; 19:4; 20:21; 26:18; Romans 1:16-17; 3:22, 25-28; 4:3, 5, 11-24; 5:1-2; 9:30-33; 10:4, 6, 9-11; 11:20; 1 Corinthians 1:21; Galatians 2:16, 20; 3:2-14, 22, 24-26; Ephesians 1:13, 19; 2:8; 3:17; Philippians 3:9; 2 Thessalonians 1:10; 2:13; 1 Timothy 1:16; 4:10; 2 Timothy 1:12; 3:15; Hebrews 4:2-3; 11:1-40; 1 Peter 1:5, 9; 2:6; 1 John 5:1, 5, 10.

Doctrine should always be built on the clearest passages of Scripture, but some people choose to ignore the obvious implications of the passages cited above, camping instead on unclear and disputed verses. The four passages that are most commonly used to dispute the assurance of the believer are John 15:6; Galatians 5:4; Hebrews 6:4-6; and James 2:18-26.

(1) *John 15:6:* "If anyone does not abide in Me, he is thrown away as a branch, and dries up; and they gather them, and cast them into the fire, and they are burned." In this context, Jesus is addressing believers on the issue of spiritual fruit, not salvation. The things that are burned are the dead works done by a believer who is not abiding in Christ. The Greek text uses the neuter gender for what is burned, and this cannot refer to the believer. A comparison with 1 Corinthians 3:11-15 illuminates this verse—the work that a believer does in the flesh will be burned at the judgment seat of Christ: "If any man's work is burned up, he shall suffer loss; but he himself shall be saved, yet so as through fire" (1 Cor. 3:15).

(2) *Galatians 5:4:* "You have been severed from Christ, you who are seeking to be justified by law; you have fallen from grace." Paul told the Galatians that Christ has set us free from the yoke of the Law (Gal. 5:1). Justification by grace is utterly incompatible with justification by law; the former is accomplished by God, and the latter

cannot be achieved by man. If a person seeks to be justified by keeping the Law, he removes himself from the principle of grace and thus abandons or falls away from grace.

(3) *Hebrews 6:4-6:* This is a very difficult passage, and many interpretations have been offered to explain it. There are some who take it to mean that a believer can lose his salvation, but few of these people realize that if the passage teaches this, it also teaches that those who lose their salvation can never get it back (and very few would want to go that far). The phrases used in verses 4 and 5 evidently refer to believers, and in context (read 5:11—6:3), this passage fits best as an exhortation for them to go on to maturity in Christ. Once a person becomes a Christian, he cannot go back and become a Christian all over again. Instead, he should grow in his relationship to God.

(4) *James 2:18-26:* It may appear that James is contradicting Paul's teaching on justification by faith (Rom. 4) when he says that "a man is justified by works, and not by faith alone" (James 2:24). However, two observations clear up the problem: (a) Paul spoke of justification before God in Romans, and this is accomplished by faith alone. James, on the other hand, is referring to the evidence before other men that one is justified, and the only real evidence would be works, not profession of faith. (b) A saving faith is a faith that works; if there are no changes in a person's life, his may be a dead faith (James 2:26).

People who have no assurance of salvation may be walking by feelings and not by faith in God's promises. But a lack of assurance may also mean that a person never really became a biblical Christian in the first place. If the Holy Spirit does not bear witness with his spirit that he is a child of God (Rom. 8:16), this witness may be absent because he is *not* a child of God. Therefore, it is unwise to give assurance to a person unless it is obvious that he is a genuine believer. Usually, if someone is unsure of where he stands with the Saviour, the best approach is to ask, "Why not make sure right now?" and invite him to pray with you to receive Christ. Even if he already knew Christ, this can be beneficial in solidifying his commitment.

Chart 68 shows the second option on the issue of assurance.

Summary and Flow Chart

When people understand the Gospel, they may wonder how anyone can be sure he isn't deceiving himself about being a Christian. Can we

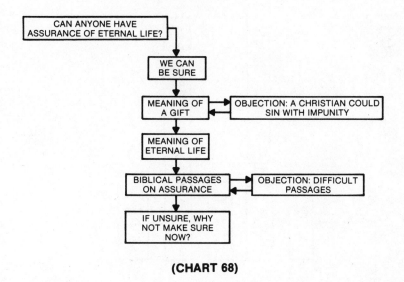

(CHART 68)

know for sure that we will go to heaven? Is there no way a Christian can lose his salvation?

Three objections to the idea of security often come up: First, can't a person stop believing? This represents a deficient understanding of the nature of faith in Christ. Second, won't certain sins disqualify a Christian? Here the confusion has to do with the nature of sin. Third, don't we have to maintain our salvation? The misunderstanding here relates to the nature of works.

The solution to the problem of assurance is to reason from what God's Word says about us, not from our feelings. Salvation is a free gift that cannot be paid for, earned, or maintained. Eternal life knows no limits, and once a person has received the life of Christ, the Scriptures are abundantly clear that no force or person can remove it from him. Some have argued from a few debated passages that salvation can be lost, but a closer analysis of these passages in their contexts reveals that they do not conflict with the clear testimony of the rest of Scripture. If someone is troubled by the matter of assurance, he can overcome his uncertainty by praying to receive Christ.

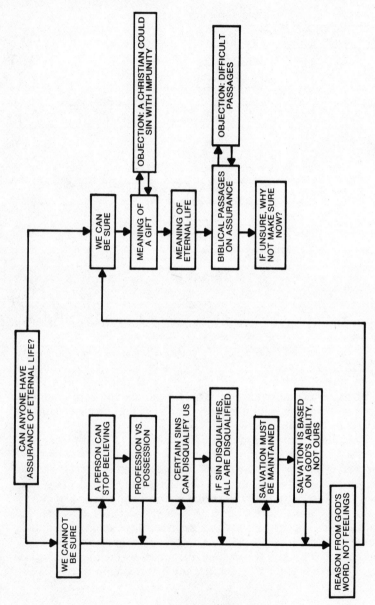

(CHART 69)

Supplemental Reading

(1) David A. DeWitt, *Answering the Tough Ones* (Moody). See chapter 3 for a brief discussion of this question.

(2) Zane C. Hodges, *The Gospel Under Siege* (Redención Viva). This outstanding treatment of faith and works deals with many difficult passages.

(3) Charles M. Horne, *Salvation* (Moody). Chapter 6 offers an in-depth analysis of the issue of the assurance of salvation.

Epilogue
Putting It into Practice

Many people can argue, but not many converse. We want this book to make you more conversant rather than more argumentative. There are occasions where we have all seen a Christian bombard a non-Christian with information in an antagnostic way. We should never be rude, for rudeness is a weak man's imitation of strength. With the message of Christ, we do not have to be defensive and hostile; the claims of Christ can withstand the onslaught of the skeptic's investigation.

Two key elements in chapter 2 for *leading* another to Christ were *love* and *listen*. Learn to be a friend to those you seek to reach. A woman who had been sharing answers with someone received a letter from that person shortly afterward. The letter read: "If you want to be a missionary, please accept this advice: be more humane. I mean more alive; cry, laugh, make mistakes, otherwise you will be just like a recorded tape saying good and right things mechanically but in an extremely cold manner. People want to find first of all a friend, a companion, and then a missionary." What a statement! How many people have we spoken to that could have written us the same letter? It may take minutes, days, months, or years before some people are ready to accept Christ. So we must continue to love them during whatever time frame it takes, and this will demonstrate whether or not we have become genuine friends.

Not only is our *approach* and *attitude* important, but so is our *ability* to answer the objections. It is curious how often people think we are geniuses just because we are the first ones able to help them in their struggle. Alexander Hamilton wrote, "Men give me some credit for genius. All the genius I have lies in this: when I have a subject at hand, I study it profoundly. Day and night it is before me. I explore it in all its bearings. My mind becomes pervaded with it. Then the efforts that I make are what people are pleased to call the fruits of genius. It is the fruit of labor and thought!"

We pray that we will all respond to the call of Christ to be ready to give an answer for the hope that is in us—an answer that will bring people to the reality of Christ. But never place your confidence in your answers. Throughout the entire process, you must walk in dependence on the power and convicting ministry of the Holy Spirit. He, not you, must convict unbelievers of the reality of sin, righteousness, and judgment (John 16:8-11). Apart from His work, your words will be void and fruitless.

Remember to be persistent in the cultivation process and be glad someone asked you to answer his questions. *Every objection is really an opportunity* to see people come to Christ.

> But you, beloved, building yourselves up on your most holy faith; praying in the Holy Spirit; keep yourselves in the love of God, waiting anxiously for the mercy of our Lord Jesus Christ to eternal life. And have mercy on some, who are doubting; save others, snatching them out of the fire; and on some have mercy with fear, hating even the garment polluted by the flesh.

> Now to Him who is able to keep you from stumbling, and to make you stand in the presence of His glory blameless with great joy, to the only God our Saviour, through Jesus Christ our Lord, be glory, majesty, dominion and authority, before all time and now and forever. Amen (Jude 20-25).

General Bibliography

The following books cover the whole range of topics related to apologetics and evangelism. We have, for the most part, selected books that are reasonably easy to follow. Philosophy of religion naturally surfaces when dealing in depth with apologetics, but the titles we have included in this area are less technical than most.

Aldrich, Joseph C. *Lifestyle Evangelism.* Portland, Oregon: Multnomah Press, 1981.

Anderson, J. N. D. *Christianity and Comparative Religion.* London: Tyndale Press, 1970.

Boa, Kenneth, *God, I Don't Understand.* Wheaton, Illinois: Victor Books, 1975.

————. *Cults, World Religions, and You.* Wheaton, Illinois: Victor Books, 1977.

Boice, James Montgomery. *Does Inerrancy Matter?* Oakland, California: International Council on Biblical Inerrancy, 1979.

————, ed. *The Foundation of Biblical Authority.* Grand Rapids: Zondervan Publishing House, 1978.

Brown, Colin, ed. *History, Criticism & Faith.* Downers Grove, Illinois: InterVarsity Press, 1976.

————. *Philosophy and the Christian Faith.* Chicago: InterVarsity Press, 1969.

Bruce, F. F. *The New Testament Documents: Are They Reliable?* 5th ed. Grand Rapids: William B. Eerdmans Publishing Company, 1960.

Carnell, Edward John. *The Case for Biblical Christianity.* Edited by Roland H. Nash. Grand Rapids: William B. Eerdmans Publishing Company, 1969.

————. *An Introduction to Christian Apologetics.* Grand Rapids: William B. Eerdmans Publishing Company, 1948.

————. *A Philosophy of the Christian Religion.* Grand Rapids: William B. Eerdmans Publishing Company, 1952.

Casserly, J. V. Langmead. *Apologetics and Evangelism.* Philadelphia: Westminster Press, 1962.

Chapman, Colin, *The Case for Christianity.* Grand Rapids: William B. Eerdmans Publishing Company, 1981.

————. *Christianity on Trial.* Wheaton: Tyndale House Publishers, 1975.

Clark, Gordon H., ed. *Can I Trust My Bible?* Chicago: Moody Press, 1963.

Clark, Robert E. D. *Science and Christianity—A Partnership.* Mountain View, California: Pacific Press Publishing Association, 1972.

Coppedge, James F. *Evolution: Possible or Impossible?* Grand Rapids: Zondervan Publishing House, 1973.

Craig, William Lane. *The Existence of God and the Beginning of the Universe.* San Bernardino, California: Here's Life Publishers, 1979.

————. *The Son Rises: Historical Evidence for the Resurrection of Jesus Christ.* Chicago: Moody Press, 1982.

Davidheiser, Bolton. *Evolution and Christian Faith.* Philadelphia: Presbyterian and Reformed Publishing Company, 1969.

DeWitt, David A. *Answering the Tough Ones.* Chicago: Moody Press, 1980.

Freeman, David Hugh. *A Philosophical Study of Religion.* Nutley, New Jersey: Craig Press, 1964.

Geisler, Norman L. *Christian Apologetics.* Grand Rapids: Baker Book House, 1976.

————, ed. *Inerrancy.* Grand Rapids: Zondervan Publishing House, 1979.

————. *Philosophy of Religion.* Grand Rapids: Zondervan Publishing House, 1974.

Geisler, Norman L. and Feinberg, Paul D. *Introduction to Philosophy*. Grand Rapids: Baker Book House, 1980.

Gerstner, John. *Reasons for Faith*. Grand Rapids: Baker Book House, 1967.

Gill, Jerry H. *The Possibility of Religious Knowledge*. Grand Rapids: William B. Eerdmans Publishing Company, 1971.

Green, Michael. *Man Alive!* Chicago: InterVarsity Press, 1967.

Guiness, Os. *The Dust of Death*. Downers Grove, Illinois: InterVarsity Press, 1973.

Gutteridge, Don J., Jr. *The Defense Rests Its Case*. Nashville: Broadman Press, 1975.

Habermas, Gary R. *The Resurrection of Jesus: An Apologetic*. Grand Rapids: Baker Book House, 1980.

Harris, R. Laird. *Inspiration and Canonicity of the Bible*. Grand Rapids: Zondervan Publishing House, 1957.

Holmes, Arthur F. *Faith Seeks Understanding*. Grand Rapids: William B. Eerdmans Publishing Company, 1971.

Hoover, Arlie J. *The Case for Christian Theism*. Grand Rapids: Baker Book House, 1976.

———. *Fallacies of Unbelief*. Abilene, Texas: Biblical Research Press, 1975.

Johnson, Cedric B. and Malony, H. Newton. *Christian Conversion: Biblical and Psychological Perspectives*. Grand Rapids: Zondervan Publishing House, 1982.

Lewis, C. S. *The Abolition of Man*. New York: Macmillan Company, 1947.

———. *God in the Dock*. Edited by Walter Hooper. Grand Rapids: William B. Eerdmans Publishing Company, 1970.

———. *Mere Christianity*. New York: Macmillan Publishing Company, 1943, 1945, 1952.

———. *Miracles, A Preliminary Study*. New York: Macmillan Publishing Company, 1947.

———. *The Problem of Pain*. New York: Macmillan Publishing Company, 1962 (1940).

Lewis, Gordon R. *Judge for Yourself*. Downers Grove, Illinois: InterVarsity Press, 1974.

———. *Testing Christianity's Truth Claims*. Chicago: Moody Press, 1976.

Little, Paul E. *How to Give Away Your Faith*. Downers Grove, Illinois: InterVarsity Press, 1966.

———. *Know Why You Believe*. Wheaton, Illinois: Victor Books, 1968.

McDill, Wayne. *Making Friends for Christ*. Nashville: Broadman Press, 1979.

McDowell, Josh. *Evidence That Demands a Verdict*. Arrowhead Springs, California: Campus Crusade for Christ, 1972.

———. *More Than a Carpenter*. Wheaton, Illinois: Tyndale House Publishers, 1977.

———. *The Resurrection Factor*. San Bernardino, California: Here's Life Publishers, 1981.

McDowell, Josh and Stewart, Don. *Answers to Tough Questions*. San Bernardino, California: Here's Life Publishers, 1980.

———. *Reasons Why Skeptics Ought to Consider Christianity*. San Bernardino, California: Here's Life Publishers, 1981.

McGinnis, Alan Loy. *The Friendship Factor*. Minneapolis: Augsburg Publishing House, 1979.

Montgomery, John Warwick, ed. *Christianity for the Tough Minded*. Minneapolis: Bethany Fellowship, 1973.

———. *Faith Founded on Fact*. Nashville: Thomas Nelson, 1978.

———, ed. *God's Inerrant Word*. Minneapolis: Bethany Fellowship, 1974.

———. *History and Christianity*. Downers Grove, Illinois: InterVarsity Press, 1964-65.

Morison, Frank. *Who Moved the Stone?* London: Faber and Faber, 1930.

Morris, Henry M. *Biblical Cosmology and Modern Science*. Nutley, New Jersey: Craig Press, 1970.

———. *Many Infallible Proofs*. San Diego: Creation-Life Publishers, 1974.

Murphree, Jon Tal. *A Loving God and a Suffering World*. Downers Grove, Illinois: InterVarsity Press, 1981.

Packer, J. I. *God Has Spoken*. Downers Grove, Illinois: InterVarsity Press, 1979.

Petersen, Jim. *Evangelism as a Lifestyle*. Colorado Springs: Navpress, 1980.

Pinnock, Clark H. *Reason Enough*. Downers Grove, Illinois: InterVarsity Press, 1980.

———. *Set Forth Your Case*. Nutley, New Jersey: Craig Press, 1967.

Prince, Matthew. *Winning Through Caring*. Grand Rapids: Baker Book House, 1981.

Purtill, Richard L. *Reason to Believe*. Grand Rapids: William B. Eerdmans Publishing Company, 1974.

Radmacher, Earl D., ed. *Can We Trust the Bible?* Wheaton, Illinois: Tyndale House Publishers, 1979.

Ramm, Bernard. *A Christian Appeal to Reason*. Waco, Texas: Word Books, 1972.

Reymond, Robert L. *The Justification of Knowledge*. Nutley, New Jersey: Presbyterian and Reformed Publishing Company, 1976.

Richardson, Don. *Eternity in Their Hearts*. Ventura, California: Regal Books, 1981.

Schaeffer, Francis A. *Escape from Reason*. Chicago: InterVarsity Press, 1968.

————. *The God Who Is There*. Chicago: InterVarsity Press, 1968.

————. *He Is There and He Is Not Silent*. Wheaton, Illinois: Tyndale House Publishers, 1972.

————. *How Should We Then Live?* Old Tappan, New Jersey: Fleming H. Revell Company, 1976.

Sylvester, Hugh. *Arguing with God*. Downers Grove, Illinois: InterVarsity Press, 1971.

Sire, James W. *The Universe Next Door*. Downers Grove, Illinois: InterVarsity Press, 1976.

Smith, A. E. Wilder. *Man's Origin, Man's Destiny*. Wheaton, Illinois: Harold Shaw Publishers, 1968.

Smith, Wilbur. *Therefore Stand*. Boston: W. A. Wilde Company, 1945.

Sproul, R. C. *If There Is a God, Why Are There Atheists?* Dimension Books. Minneapolis: Bethany Fellowship, 1974.

————. *Objections Answered*. Regal Books. Glendale, California: Gospel Light Publications, 1978.

Stevenson, Kenneth E. and Habermas, Gary R. *Verdict on the Shroud*. Ann Arbor: Servant Books, 1981.

Stott, John R. W. *Basic Christianity*. 2nd ed. Downers Grove, Illinois: InterVarsity Press, 1971.

Tenney, Merrill C. *The Reality of the Resurrection*. New York: Harper & Row, 1963.

Thurman, L. Duane. *How to Think about Evolution*. Downers Grove, Illinois: InterVarsity Press, 1978.

Van Til, Cornelius. "Apologetics." Unpublished class syllabus, Westminster Theological Seminary, n.d.

————. *Christian-Theistic Evidences*. Phillipsburg, New Jersey: Presbyterian and Reformed Publishing Company, 1978 (1975).

————. *The Defense of the Faith*. 3rd ed. Philadelphia: Presbyterian and Reformed Publishing Company, 1967.

Wenham, John W. *The Goodness of God*. Downers Grove, Illinois: InterVarsity Press, 1974.

Williams, Rheinallt Nantlais. *Faith, Facts, History, Science—and How They Fit Together*. Wheaton, Illinois: Tyndale House Publishers, 1973.

Wilson, Clifford A. *Rocks, Relics and Biblical Reliability*. Christian Free University Curriculum. Grand Rapids: Zondervan Publishing House, 1977.

Wolterstorff, Nicholas. *Reason Within the Bounds of Religion*. Grand Rapids: William B. Eerdmans Publishing Company, 1976.

Wood, Barry. *Questions Non-Christians Ask*. Old Tappan, New Jersey: Fleming H. Revell Company, 1977.

Yamauchi, Edwin. *The Stones and the Scriptures*. Philadelphia: J. P. Lippincott Company, 1972.

Yancey, Philip. *Where Is God When It Hurts?* Grand Rapids: Zondervan Publishing House, 1977.